Paul Durcan

Praise in Which
I Live and Move and
Have my Being

Harvill *Secker*
LONDON

Published by Harvill Secker 2012

2 4 6 8 10 9 7 5 3 1

First published in Great Britain in 2012 by
HARVILL SECKER
Random House
20 Vauxhall Bridge Road
London SW1V 2SA

www.randomhouse.co.uk

Addresses for companies within The Random House Group Limited can be found at: www.randomhouse.co.uk/offices.htm

The Random House Group Limited Reg. No. 954009

A CIP catalogue record for this book is available from the British Library

ISBN 9781846556272

The Random House Group Limited supports The Forest Stewardship Council (FSC®), the leading international forest certification organisation. Our books carrying the FSC label are printed on FSC® certified paper. FSC is the only forest certification scheme endorsed by the leading environmental organisations, including Greenpeace. Our paper procurement policy can be found at www.randomhouse.co.uk/environment

Typeset by Palimpsest Book Production Limited, Falkirk, Stirlingshire

Printed and bound in Great Britain by
Clays Ltd, St Ives plc

PRAISE IN WHICH
I LIVE AND MOVE
AND HAVE MY BEING

Despite all, when all hope is lost, what actually reappears is the motherly image of a oneness recovered at last: God is only father when he promises a mother's love.

André Manaranche, *O Espírito e a Mulher*
São Paulo, 1976

Acknowledgements

Special acknowledgements are due to Patsey Murphy, editor of *The Irish Times Magazine*, in which versions of five of these poems were published on 24 December 2010.

Versions of six other poems were published in the *Sunday Independent, The Moth, News Four, Poetry Ireland, Boulevard Magenta, Shine On* (edit. Pat Boran) and *Poetry London*.

First and last I wish to thank Dr Clíona Ní Ríordáin for her advice, patience and practical criticism in the preparation of the manuscript of this book.

to
Deirdre Madden and Harry Clifton
with affection and gratitude

Contents

On Glimpsing a Woman in Hodges
   Figgis Bookshop in Dublin 1

To Brian Friel on his Eightieth Birthday 4

The Lamb around My Neck 6

Nature 8

The Most Extraordinary Innovation 9

Maureen Durcan 11

The Art Institute of Chicago 12

Idolatry 13

October Early Morning Haircut 16

The Ballyshannon Trucker 19

Thinking about Suicide 21

Self-Pity 23

"The Spirit that Lives Alone" 24

Woman Lying On a Wall 26

Post-haste to John Moriarty, Easter Sunday, 2007 27

Death of a Corkman 32

On the First Day of June 33

★   ★   ★

The Boy from Belarus 35

Toowoomba Father's Day Mystery Tour 2007 38

Traces of the Sacred 40

How I Envy the Homeless Man 41

Nuala O'Faolain 43

Paris, Bloomsday 2009 44

ICI REPOSE VINCENT VAN GOGH 1853–1890 46

The Birth of Arthur Lev Drummond, 25 May 2008 ... 49

Meeting Kathleen and Philippe Bernard 51

Le Petit Journal Jazz Club, Saint Michel,
    10 June 2009 53

Petit Déjeuner with Breda 56

In the Luxembourg Gardens in the Rain 58

Christmas in Paris 60

The Road to Vétheuil 2009 62

★   ★   ★

Death of a Miniaturist 63

Today I Met David Kelly, Actor, in the Street 64

June and Ivor 66

The Café Java 68

Charles Brady, Painter 70

To Dympna Who Taught Me Online Banking 72

The Lady in Weir's 74

The Recession 77

Morning Ireland, Be Warned! 79

Mother and Child, Merrion Square West 80

Forefinger 82

Meeting the Poet 84

Kate La Touche 85

A Man Besotted by his Batch 87

Michael Longley's Last Poetry Reading 89

To be Ella or Not to be Ella 91

A Cast-Iron Excuse 92

Sandymount Green 93

★   ★   ★

Achill Island Postman 94

1950s Boat 95

At the Grave of Michael Carr 97

Slievemore Cemetery Headstones 102

Caught Out 103

The Children of the Land of Dreams 104

Oaxaca 106

At the True Romance Cinema 109

Life Guard 110

The Clothes Line 111

Achill Island Tourist Spots No. 6 112

Flotsam 114

Michael Dan Gallagher Down
    at the Sound, 10.30 a.m. 115

Passing Through 116

Sunny Hill 118

Time Stole Away 120

Woman, Outside 121

Diversity 123

        ★   ★   ★

Bernie 125

Sandymount Strand Keeping Going 126

On Being Collected at the Railway Station
    in Ennis 129

Sick of Acquaintances Who are Know-Alls 131

Staring Out the Window Three Weeks after his Death   132

Old Lady in a Wheelbarrow, Haiti, January 2010 133

Wild Life on the Grand Canal 135

Love at Last Sight 138

The Old Guy in the Aisle Seat 139

Aristotle with a Bust of Homer 141

Valdi 143

The Docker at Eighty Walking his Dog
    in the Snow 146

Stage Four 149

Free Travel Pass 153

The Annual January Nervous Breakdown 156

PRAISE IN WHICH
I LIVE AND MOVE
AND HAVE MY BEING

On Glimpsing a Woman in Hodges Figgis Bookshop in Dublin

I am standing in line at the checkout of Hodges Figgis
    bookshop in Dublin
On a Monday morning in July
When I spot a woman pluck a book off a counter, fling it
    open,
And start to write on the title page
With a retractable ball-point biro. She repeats the action.
    She repeats it again.
I am wrong-footed.
All the more so
Because she's an unlikely-looking book psychopath.
Tall, blonde ponytail, blue denim outfit, country-and-
    western boutique style.
Although it costs me my place, I drop out of line
And slope around the book counter like a sheepdog on a
    recce
Wet-eyed to identify the title of the book and what is she
    writing in it.
Perching on my hind legs I see
It's entitled *Champagne Kisses* by Amanda Brunker
And in each copy in huge characters she is inscribing the
    words "Amanda Brunker",
Inscribing them with such concentrated flourishes as if the
    book was the Book of Kells.

She turns around to a bookshop assistant and remarks in a
    low, husky voice:
"Oh I was just passing and I saw my books on your shelf
So I thought I'd sign them for you – okey-dokey?"
Cool! The author herself! Amanda Brunker!
The first thing I think is that Amanda Brunker is mortal.
The second thing I think is that Amanda Brunker is a
    looker.
The third thing I think is: Roll over Jane Austen!
What cunning, what audacity, what breezy, cool arrogance!
After she rides out of the shop on her white bronco
I take down her book and read the first paragraph:
Why did I have a full Irish for breakfast?
It's as if I am mechanically programmed to make the wrong
    decision
at every available opportunity.
Such candour, such detail, such insight, such information!
And all in the first paragraph.
The story of my own life.
Why did I park on the fourth floor of the multi-storey car
    park
When I knew if I parked on the sixth floor
I'd have direct access to the supermarket?
It's as if . . .
Why did I get up at 9.30 a.m.
When I could have stayed in bed all morning?
It's as if . . .
Why did I agree a year ago to participate next week
In the Poetry Marathon at the World Ploughing
    Championships in Darlington

2

When I knew it would cause me nothing but humiliation
    and exhaustion?
It's as if . . .
Why did I have a cappuccino in Starbucks when I knew I
    could have got
A far tastier, cheaper and more agreeable cappuccino
In the adjacent Topaz filling station?
It's as if . . .
Amanda, thank you for putting into words
What makes me tick. Methinks I tick too much.
On the other hand, soon I'll not be ticking at all.
Go for it, Amanda Brunker, go for it!

To Brian Friel on his
Eightieth Birthday

Irina – a bitterly attractive young middle-aged French
    woman
Originally from the Vaucluse but long resident in Paris –
Not only had not the slightest interest in me
But had a pointedly sensual technique of making that clear,
Pursing her lips in abstract formulations of kisses.
But as well as her golden tresses and her buck teeth
She was affectionate, thoughtful, hospitable
And seeing how sheep-astray I was in Paris
She invited me to supper in her apartment in the 19th
With a male laboratory technician and a female civil
    servant.
I felt like an old ram looking into a plate-glass shop
    window
Unable not to see my horned visage peering back out at
    me,
Pining to crash through it.
Anyway . . . that night in her roof-top apartment in the
    19th *arrondissement*
I asked to go to the toilet and traversing her hall in
    twilight
I entered her tiny bedroom by mistake;
There on the wall at the foot of her super king-size bed,
Her super king-size bed in her minuscule bedroom,
There on the pristine white wall

Was a floor-to-ceiling poster in green and black,
Gigantic black characters of the alphabet on pure green
  ground,
Expertly framed in walnut. They read:
THE AFTERNOON IN DUBLIN BRIAN FRIEL KISSED ME ON
  THE CHEEK.

The Lamb around My Neck

One night in Connemara Nestor Thornton stopped me:
"Jump into the car and come with me."
Nestor would have been about twenty-eight. I was sixteen.
He was a jack of all trades, including a hackney driver,
But first and last Nestor was a sheep farmer.
On no road known to man
He drove up the side of a mountain
Telling me his plan.
On a black, moonless, starless night
When he got out of the car leaving the headlights on
I'd stand at the head of two drystone walls
And when he'd herd a lamb towards me
I'd hurl myself through the air,
Body-tackling it, and he'd tie up its legs.

So it came to pass that I found myself
Walking back down a mountain to a car
With a lamb around my neck,
Gripping tight a pair of lamb's legs in each hand,
But when I came to the open boot of the car
I kept on walking – I kept on walking
Talking to myself
Down the drystone gauntlets of the years
Through byways in London, Moscow, Toronto, Hiroshima,
    Galway,
Paris, Rio, Jerusalem, Invercargill, Keel, Scarborough,

Skopje, Warsaw, Nova Scotia, Berlin, Tyneside,
Vancouver, Luxembourg, Perugia, Funchal, Mainz,
Scunthorpe, Antigonish, Edenderry, The Hague, Ilkley,
Portmuck, Rotterdam, Limerick, Brighton, Cork,
Singapore, Corner Brook, Brisbane, Killorglin,
Stockholm, Dublin, Belfast, Glasgow, Gort, Dumfries,
Saskatoon, Fortaleza, Chicago, Tbilisi, Ballymahon,
Westport, New York, Ann Arbor, Boyle, Lourmarin, Achill,
Through knacker's yards and university cloisters,
Gutters and podiums, dosshouses and tea rooms, dives and
    idylls
With the lamb around my neck,
Until not even in the county hospital tonight
Can the ward sister be bothered to separate us.
In a bed in the corner of a swarming public ward
I fall into a deep, restful sleep with the lamb around my
    neck.

Nature

I was sitting up in bed in the ward at dawn
When the man in the bed opposite sat up also –
He had been wheeled in during the night
From the operating theatre –
Only he was not a man, he was an otter,
A most distinguished-looking otter,
Sideburns, handlebar mustachios.
He sat bolt upright for five minutes,
Knowing full well that I was over here
Staring at him goggle-eyed.
Then he chose to utter to me
In a light baritone Somerset voice:
"Let me introduce myself, feller.
I am the Official Archival Handmade
Paper-Maker to Her Majesty the Queen."
While I ingested this morsel of zoological classification
He slid out of bed and sloped out the ward
Trailing his scar tissue on the parquet behind him,
Wads of handmade paper of a sumptuous fabric.
Down below in the lamp-lit car park outside the ward
    window
A short, lightly built, black-corduroyed oncologist was
    half-running,
His arms chock-a-block with files, embracing them.

The Most Extraordinary Innovation

What an extraordinary thing it is to be nursed!
Ordinarily I'd be skulking in my den!
Nursed! All of a sudden to be taken in hand,
In the public ward of a general hospital,
Mayo General Hospital in Castlebar,
Nurtured, nourished by a female stranger!
Can you believe that it happens?
Human nature being what it is:
Oppressive, manipulative, malicious, callous?
Kindness, support, gentleness, humour,
Warmth, conversation, food, sleep,
Conviviality, *confiance*, companionship.
For me these are freakish things.
Whether you're a boy of thirteen from a
    dysfunctional family
Or a man of sixty-four living alone like a wounded
    animal,
To have women at your hospital bedside
Emptying buckets of tenderness over your head,
Hosing you down with solicitude,
Is something ridiculously out of the ordinary.
Prayer would seem abstract by comparison.
Did Virgil or Dante ever witness such scenes?
You cry out: "I am not used to this!
Hold on! Wait a minute!
What have I done to merit such treatment?

All I have done is to get myself injured."
But she cannot wait, she is busy,
Twenty-six other patients to attend to before the
    Angelus
As she gives you an intravenous injection.
Whether you like it or not
She injects you with smiles also
And all the while you lie there transfixed
Like a cornered hedgehog.
Her eyes run up and down your hairy, lumpy, veiny
    body
Like rabbits in a sandhill.
To nurse! To be nursed!
To be nursed back to health or unto death.
From the Latin: *to nourish*.
Slim, sturdy, buxom nourishers, almost anonymous:
Teresa, Joan, Niamh, Anne-Marie, Helena, Louise,
    Nicola, Marie.
Of all the innovations of human kind
Nursing is the most extraordinary innovation of all.

Maureen Durcan

A grain of sand I am blown on to a
Clump of heather and I see
Alight large above me a butterfly
With black and orange stripes –
It's Auntie Maureen aged ninety-four
Smiling down upon me
And she is saying
"While you were sleeping, Paul, I died.
Isn't it the most glorious morning!"

21 September 2003
  Westport

The Art Institute of Chicago

Small curly-headed black boy in awe beholding the
    conveyor belt!
His tall father, having placed their lunch tray on it,
Turns his back to walk away, but Small Curly Head
Stands transfixed staring at the disappearing tray,
Disappearing offstage into where? Into whom?
This is the secret of the Art Institute of Chicago,
Known only to the child poet.

He hops up and lies flat on his back on the belt.
Within seconds he also has disappeared.
His tall father turns around to hold his hand
Only to find his curly-headed small boy not there!
Not even the side of his head.
"Eddie!" he cries out in awe. "Eddie!"
I explain to him about the conveyor belt and the
    kitchens.

He rages. The woman on the till
Instructs him to sit down while she phones the kitchens.
When Small Curly Head reappears
Between two kitchen hands he is smiling
And he races to his raging father
And hugs him, clawing him,
The milky grooves of his stainless-steel paws perspiring
    with calf-love.

Idolatry

Meeting by accident on a winter's night
High in the rooftops of Georgian Dublin,
She from the capital city of Tbilisi,
I from the capital city of Dublin,
We became fast friends,
Cor loquitor ad cor,
Heart speaking to heart,
Joined together at the eyes;
Laughter and silence our freedom ties;
Levity, sobriety, probity.

She wrote cards to me that I left her "breathless",
Knowing, as she did, that I had been left
    "breathless" by her.
That first night as she flew out the door
Down the granite steps to a waiting taxi
She flicked her head round and looking me in the
    eye,
With mirth and affection hummed
From "Desolation Row":
And Ezra Pound and T. S. Eliot
Fighting in the captain's tower . . .
So much we had laughed, so much.
"So long. See you soon. So long."

Two months later on a balmy Wednesday in
    February
After a three hour lunch
In the National Gallery
I walked her back to her place of work.
"Goodbye. See you soon. Take care."
I did not cross the street with her
For fear of her thinking
I might be clinging to her.
(Actually I was clinging to her like mad –
Running in front of her every five metres
Like Groucho Marx, bowing to her,
Letting on to be funny, pretending
To be godlike-blasé, and she laughed
And the more she laughed the more I believed
In every preposterous improvisation of my soul
Until at last I flung myself down on the pavement
And she had no choice but to step across me.
"O Paolo!" she cried. "O Paolo! *Ciao!*")

I watched her in her long black overcoat,
Low black heels, silver-grey scarf,
Shy eyes bowed,
Gain the other pavement and then –
What did she do but glance back at me
Through the hurtling traffic
With a look of horror in her eyes,
A look of such horror
I recognised it instantly,
The same grief-stricken horror

Shrieking from the eyes of the boy child
Bitten by a lizard
In the picture by Caravaggio –
Only she was not a boy child
But a 43-year-old woman
In the prime of her life,
Her eyes out on stalks,
Her mouth prised open
As if she were about to asphyxiate
In a bog-hole of pitch-black concupiscence,
Bitten by an older man,
By some ancient venom in him,
Some murderous instinct in him.

That was six months ago. Why O why O why?
I have asked myself over and over.
Was it maybe because I quoted St Augustine
To her from his *Confessions*?
Inqueatum est cor nostrum donec
    requiescat in Te:
Restless is my heart until it rests in Thee.

October Early Morning Haircut

In the barber shop early this morning in Baggot
    Street the barber
Turned out to be an Algerian Berber – a young
    man descended
From the original, indigenous peoples of Algeria
Who populated that immense territory long, long
    before
The Arabs and much later the French.
He was a tall, dark, curly-headed young man
Dressed all in black,
Quiet, not garrulous, reserved, reticent,
Concentrating on the job in hand,
My hoary, old, white head overgrown
Like my garden and everything else in my life.
He snipped and trimmed in meditative silence.
I mentioned a recent murder in the neighbourhood
(A so-called "road-rage murder"
In which an Irish motorist had snatched a hurley
    stick from his car boot
And beat the brains out of the other driver – an
    Englishman).
One topic led to another,
Which of course is the beauty of conversation,
Its purpose and meaning, and next thing
The Algerian Berber barber was telling me

How only the other morning he'd been cutting the
    hair
Of an archaeology professor, and how this client
Had stated that it may have been the Berbers of
    Algeria
Who 6,000 years ago BC
Constructed Newgrange – the most famous
    monument in Ireland,
Fabled and fabulous, older than the pyramids,
A vast circular tumulus that to this day
Has always looked more like the creation
Of people from outer space.
"Yes," responded my barber lugubriously but
    proudly,
"But you see, sir, the Berbers *are* from outer space."
I stared into the long looking glass at his dark face
Wide-eyed over my white head,
Delicately twirling his scissors.
"Yes," he repeated solemnly, almost inaudibly,
"My people – the Berbers of Algeria –
Are people from outer space."
Nodding his head, he added:
"Are you a pensioner, sir?"
The first time in my life
Anyone had ever asked me that question.
"Well, as a matter of fact,
Yes, I am a pensioner!"
"In that case, sir," he smiled eagerly, gently,
Showing me all of his snow-white white teeth,
"It will be six – not sixteen – euro."

17

Out on the street for the rest of the morning
I had to keep restraining myself
From breaking out into frolics,
From playing hopscotch with myself.
What would the cultural police
Texting and emailing their victims –
Tweeting and twittering –
Have to say about a 66-year-old white-haired man
Playing hopscotch with himself on the streets of
    Dublin city?

The Ballyshannon Trucker

Crouching outside the Café Java with a cappuccino
On a chilly, breezy morning in early February
(*That man* will do anything for human company)
When who do I see strolling towards me out of
    twenty-five years ago
As out of the middle of a phone call
Or out of a vision in the desert in New Mexico
Or out of the Dry Cleaners of a previous era
Or out of the black shawl of the Spanish Arch
Or out of a roadside café in the Highlands
Or from the far side of a bar that no longer exists
But the Ballyshannon Trucker in the same gear:
Blue jeans, blue baseball cap, black leather jacket,
Only maybe looking younger – white hair and all.

Like all great truckers – a quiet guy
Who lives for his wife and his two daughters;
Who works harder than almost any man I've
    known.
"Will you have a coffee?" I sing. "I will," he smiles.
There and then, with no big production, no intro,
    no ado,
We chat about only the things that matter
When you're high in the cab in the depths of
    Newfoundland:
The Mounties on their walkie-talkies telling you

That the road to Corner Brook is blocked with
    snow,
Ditto Gander, Goose Bay, St John's.
He suggests to me a difference between what it
    means
To be spiritual and to be religious:
"Breathe Deep, Heavy Trucking, Keep Moving."

As we stand up to shake hands to say farewell
He explains to me also how his wife Marie has
    asked him
To buy "one large head of cauliflower".
How proud he is of his errand and of her.
"Marie, Marie, hold on tight." And down they went.
A Tourmakeady girl with her Sam Shepard.
In the mountains of your dread, there you feel free.
Holding hands they careered down the fields and
    the walls
Into the towns and the cities and by ferry and air
Crossed over the oceans until he started driving
And she came home and a child was born.
Adieu to thee, my Ballyshannon Trucker.
"Breathe Deep, Heavy Trucking, Keep Moving."

Thinking about Suicide

Although I may never commit suicide
I spend parts of each day thinking about suicide –
Thinking about how I lack the courage to do it.

I wake in the morning with 60 per cent depression.
That's how it remains for the whole day,
Except for the odd occasion in a year

In the doorway or on the street I meet by chance
For a few minutes a woman passing-by
Who has the time to stop and talk for three
    minutes

Or five minutes or even sometimes seven or eight
    minutes,
Who rocks back on her heels in her pink, hooped
    skirt
With laughter, no matter what the topic.

Depression and despair are two different states
Of mind, not having a lot in common.
Although I have 60 per cent depression, I do not
    despair.

I do not see eye to eye with Samuel Beckett
Who disapproved of suicide and who promulgated
The doctrine of "going on" for the sake of
   "going on".

Estranged from my family, if I do not soon
Take my own life, others will take it from me –
Hooded males with knives in their tracksuits

Or medics in their scrubs prancing corridors
Or cowpat-faced ward sisters smirking
Or ice-cold proprietors of old people's homes.

How is it that you do not see it, Samuel,
That I do not want to go on for the sake of
   going on –
Seeing the same old, tired-out impressionist
   paintings again and again?

Men are such po-faced bores.
Each one of them an editor-in-chief.
I want to stand still by the water's edge.

I want to hold a woman's hand for the last time.
I want to fill my pockets with Palaeozoic stones.
I want to open my eyes.

Self-Pity

I am Self-Pity – the most red-hot woman in Ireland.
Younger than time, older than eternity.
All raddle, all lacquer, all scent.
Great is my glory
I who can turn a man into a 24/7 ghost of himself.

I am Self-Pity – the Queen Bee of the Irish Sea.
I have only to squint at a half-decent man
To make him hold his head in his hands,
Make him put his fist through a pane of glass,
Make him stamp his feet.

I am Self-Pity – the Black Madonna of Ireland.
Great was my education and great my family.
I who with my fabulous loneliness,
Demanding total, exclusive, absolute love,
Reduced a half-decent man to smithereens.

I am Self-Pity – the most red-hot woman in Ireland.
Younger than time, older than eternity.
All raddle, all lacquer, all scent.
Great is my glory
I who can turn a man into a 24/7 ghost of himself.

"The Spirit that Lives Alone"

The lock gates of the Grand Canal at Baggot Street
  Bridge,
Grassy banks, birch trees, poplars, copper beeches,
All my life the domain of solitary men and solitary
  women:
Patrick Kavanagh, Owen Walsh, Helen Moloney,
  Frances Bunch Moran, Michael Kane, Jack. B. Yeats
And now today late on a Saturday afternoon in July
Behind Kavanagh's seat – the one with the poem
  carved on it –
O commemorate me where there is water,
Canal water preferably –
The flames of a fire under a low-branched sycamore
Streaking red and yellow, and in the shadows of the
  tree trunk,
Sitting up against it, gazing into the flames,
Over hunched-up knees,
A man not much more than forty,
Coal-black hair, gleaming white teeth.
Is he from Warsaw or Walkinstown?
Clontarf or the Czech Republic?
Passers-by pause to stare at him, but not for long,
Perturbed by the ferocity of his gaze or by their own
  timidity.
Why are we so surprised, fearful, outraged?
As if the man has committed a heinous crime

By resorting to the ancient rite of lighting a fire
In a public place under a tree to placate the gods.
The whites of his eyes leap in and out of the flames
As it dawns on him at five o'clock in the afternoon
That he *is* Napoleon on the island of St Helena,
Pacing the rampart, a man of destiny, fated to fall
    apart.
No one should think in prose who finds his way
Into the original, terminal isolation of his mortal soul.

Woman Lying On a Wall

after Lowry and Longley

Hands clasped under her breasts, handbag around her
  neck,
Feet in grey brogues dangling, eyes curved
In spite of passers-by curving around her.
Maybe she is sleeping, maybe she is not sleeping.
She is not askew with anxiety
To run for the next bus, or to run for anything.

"It was hard getting out of bed this morning,
Hard waiting for the bus,
Hard waiting in line in the hospital for radiotherapy.
But that was this morning and now it is
  mid-afternoon
Taking a catnap in one of those slivers of sunlight
That fall our way in this part of the world.
I don't mind death itself, it's the dying part I don't
  fancy.
O Maestro, stand to, flick your trowel, delineate me:
Woman Lying On a Wall. Medieval. Local Limestone."

Post-haste to John Moriarty, Easter Sunday, 2007

My Dear John of Moyvane,
Author of *Serious Sounds*,
On Good Friday in Westport,
A day of pure sunlight,
In the newsagents on the Mall
I heard the news
That the Stations of the Cross
Would be at three o'clock
In a valley in the mountains,
Mám Éan,
The Pass of the Birds.

I got a lift to Mám Éan from Dr John Keane,
The back road past Drummin,
Down the Erriff river,
On up through the oasis of Leenane,
Up along the Killary fjord,
Past the tiny tented chapel
Of Our Lady of the Wayside
At Creevagh,
Pegged down on the moor
Above Wittgenstein's cottage,
Down into the Inagh Valley,
The skulls of the mountains the same
As they were before pre-history began.

The mountain path
Was the bed of a winter stream,
Stony, slippery,
All clefts, pebbles
Being washed away
By streams of pilgrims,
Brisk hill-walkers,
Middle-aged worriers,
Undaunted young marrieds,
Separated spouses
Scampering in desperation,
Children asking questions,
Old people on their hind legs.

I crept past
Two aged, crippled sisters
From Camus
Talking in Irish
Royally,
And I could hear you, John,
Among their cadences,
Their luscious crevices,
Your torrential whispers,
*Et egressus est Jesus cum discipulis suis trans
     torrentem Cedron.*

There you were, John,
Grasping your staff
In the sun and the wind,
Your iconic head,

The birth-pangs of the universe
Reproduced in your hair,
Furrowed furlongs
Of your face terraced
In suffering and joy,
Greeting your creatures,
Lapwing, lark, lamb,
At 1,200 feet
On the saddle of the pass,
The islands of Connemara to the west,
The plains of the Joyce Country to the east.
Christ Jesus, how are you?
I bring the thunder in my right hand!

Up above us in the mouth of a cave
Swayed a white-haired,
Brown-faced man
In white shirt, blue jeans:
Joe John Mac an Iomaire of Cill Chiaráin,
Intoning the lament,
In the sean nós,
Caoineadh na dTrí Mhuire,
His hands on his hips,
The stones of Connemara
Shining in his cheekbones,
The stones of Palestine,
The stones of Greece.

Alongside the keener,
The Jesuit soldier,
Father Micheál MacGréill,
In a low, fierce voice
Proclaiming the Stations of the Cross
"For the people of the Middle East"
And declaring to us that the good man
Always will be destroyed by evil men:
"Jesus falls for the second time:
He is getting weaker and weaker."

I came back down the mountain and I found
Brendan Flynn of Clifden
Sitting in the grass by the side of the road
In the Long Acre, grieving.
He told me of last Tuesday night
At your bedside in Kerry.

Back on the Mall of Westport
A river undresses itself
Between walled banks
Under young limes leafing
On the North Mall,
On the South Mall;
On facing seats
Old ladies soldiering their agony
With girlish pluck;
The sun thrice dancing on the mountain peak
(As my father always said it would do).

In the name of the Risen Gardener, John, good
   morning.
Good morning, Mary. Good morning, James.
Good morning, Lydia. Good morning, Eileen.
I am in the town of Westport and you are Easter
   over Croagh Patrick.
Molfaidh mé i gCamus tú.
I will praise you in Camus.

Death of a Corkman

in memoriam Junior Daly

He was a place not a time:
He was a street corner in rush hour,
His laughing eyes looking sideways;
He was a cigarette cupped in his left hand
In a force five gale on Grand Parade;
He was a pair of eyes twinkling
In the crook of his elbow;
He was a man walking home from work;
He minded children;
He was a follower of the Munster rugby team;
He was a reader of the *Evening Echo* and every
     book that had ever been written
On the First World War and the Second World
     War;
He carried under his arm the headlines
Of the history of the world in the twentieth
     century;
He was a private man in a public place;
He was a glass of wine in a hand every hair of
     whose wrist
His woman knew as she knew every willow tree
     along the river in Sunday's Well
Walking at evening
On a rope bridge made for two.
He was a Corkman.

On the First Day of June

I was walking behind Junior Daly's coffin
Up a narrow winding terraced street
In Cork city in the rain on the first day of June
When my mobile phone went off in my pocket:
Marie Hughes in her hushed voice informing me
That twelve minutes ago John Moriarty had died
In his house on the mountain in Kerry.
By the time the cortège had reached the top of the
    hill
And we were entering the west door of the North
    Cathedral
Junior Daly had been joined by John Moriarty;
Together they stood to one side of the high altar,
Watching us walk up the centre aisle;
The caretaker of North Presentation Primary
    School,
The philosopher of Mangerton Mountain;
The short man with the crisp moustache,
The tall man with the mane of grey hair;
The short man with the film-star looks,
The tall man with the Indian-chief looks;
The two of them pursued, hunted, harried,
    cornered
By the same Rottweiler of cancer,
All the same terror and humiliation,
All the same being-devoured-into-bits.

Beginning slowly to spin, accelerating,
Spinning as if he was totally out of it,
As if he was totally in the grip of the hammer.

Big fat boy from Belarus
Spinning faster than a Formula One racing car
Gone out of control,
About to vanish up into the bleachers of the
    stadium,
Never to be seen again
On this side of the cosmos,
About to evaporate in a sliver of samurai sky,
About to expire once for all in Osaka,
About to consummate his own nothingness.

What boys surely are always doing or wanting to
    be doing.
Only at the last moment letting go of his
    hammer,
Yet maintaining his foothold,
Staying on his feet inside the circle,
The needle of his groin quivering
Inside the screened-off cage of his soul.

The commentator was hyperventilating,
Howling hyperbole.
But the boy was laughing. He knew what he'd
    done
Without even having to look up from his spot,
Without even having to bother to track

The trajectory of his hammer-throw,
To witness its upshot,
His missile landing out beyond anyone else in the
   known world.

I in my poky sofa in a motel room in Brisbane
Under a dying sixty-watt bulb on a night with
   no future,
I laughed also at the spectacle of such beauty,
   such innocence,
Such boyish optimism, his black hair in his eyes.
His name − I googled it next day
In an office in a warehouse in Fortitude Valley −
Was Ivan Tsikhan,
The boy from Belarus.

29 August 2007

Toowoomba Father's Day
Mystery Tour 2007

I am seventy-nine, not a pick on me,
A dairy farmer in Toowoomba.
Got all my gnashers still.
Finest town in Australia, Toowoomba.
The Garden City, they call it.
Born there. I will die there.
At least I hope I will die there.
Here I am today in bloody Brisbane
All because to please a wife
I agreed to accompany her today
On the Toowoomba Father's Day Mystery
    Tour.

Up I was at 4 a.m. – a Sunday morning, for
    Christ's sake! –
To climb into a coach not knowing
Where I was going, to please a wife.
Mystery to me why I did it.
I ask you, mate!
Where do I wind up? In bloody Brisbane.
Squatting on a wall on the banks of the river.
Look at all that bloody water!
She's walked off in a stink on the boardwalk.
Where are *you* from anyway?
Ireland?

No offence, mate.
Tell you something for nothing, mate.
If I get back to Toowoomba tonight
I will never leave Toowoomba again
Not even if it's to please the hundred
    thousand bloody wives of Osama
    whatever-his-name-is.
Enjoy your stay in Australia, mate.

2 September 2007

Traces of the Sacred

On the esplanade of the Pompidou Centre,
That vast, sloping, paved embankment
Conceived by the architects as part of the Centre,
A middle-aged woman is lying on her side,
Her knees tucked up, four tightly packed
Carrier bags parked neatly beside her.
Nearby mime artists are going through their paces
While high up above across the top of the Centre
Is emblazoned the logo of the new, big, art show:
TRACES OF THE SACRED.
Is she a solo act or part of the show –
Herself also a "trace of the sacred"?
Or is she a homeless woman on her last legs –
A profane gatecrasher in the sacred world of art?

How I Envy the Homeless Man

How I envy the homeless man
Who sleeps on the pavement under my window
His self-containment, his composure,
His faith in his own fate.

So wholly does he trust in his fate
That when I open my window at 3 a.m.
I am looking down into his face asleep
Like an infant in its cot.

His hands are palm-open to the night sky
Yet like an infant also
His sleeping face fills me with fear,
Fear of his fate.

When I look out again at 10.30 a.m.
I am dismayed to see his nest empty
But then he appears again at the street corner.
His unmistakeable bespectacled figure

Armed with a baguette and a bottle of wine
He climbs back into his cardboard
Sitting up with bread and wine
He opens a book: *The Da Vinci Code.*

If I had a gram of his integrity,
His courage, his independence,
Even in these last years of my life
I might make a go of it — sing

As I have always yearned to sing
The song of my silence, the song
Of the men and women I love
Of the places that make me feel at home.

Nuala O'Faolain

When the news of her death broke
I walked across the Luxembourg Gardens
To the Gallimard bookshop
At 15 Boulevard Raspail;
Stood gazing in the window
At the display of her books:
On s'est déjà vu quelque part?
All her French titles.
In the midst of it all
A large head-and-shoulders photograph
Of her laughing lustily
In the limelight of her fame,
A teardrop
On the shores of eternity.

10 May 2008

Paris, Bloomsday 2009

Sloping around the Luxembourg Gardens at five in
   the afternoon:
Infant and child riding giraffe and antelope;
Grumpy, placid men playing boules under chestnuts;
A middle-aged couple trying to accomplish it on a
   bench.

My sole aim this 16th of June –
To contrive to circulate around Baudelaire's bust:
"A teardrop's dying fall
Once more on the shores of eternity."

At long last I arrive back at the gates
Where the ancient madame selling ice cream
Greets me as her long-lost grandson,
Who here last year lost his sack

Only to have it found and returned to him
By her – his long-lost maternal grandmother:
Madame Marguerite Saint-Lazare,
3 rue Gay Lussac.

Bon après-midi, Madame!
Framboise, une boule, s'il vous plaît.

I sit on a bollard in the shade,
Watching my grandmother at work;
Scooping up flavours from the fridge;
Topping up cones for all-comers.

Smacking my lips, my tongue fulfilled,
I traipse uphill to the rue des Irlandais;
Up the steep hill of rue Royer Collard,
Hard on the heels of a small schoolgirl

Carrying a sack on her back
Bigger than herself. In her daydream
She is tiptoeing stepping stones, humming;
I halt to give her space and time.

When I die I will have Space on my plate.
Oh my poor man! My poor, poor man!
I will miss Time but with such Space
Who can complain? Not me, not Bloom.

Bloom, my old flower, her voice!
Life is an ice cream in a summer breeze!
I regret almost everything!
Stand and rejoice!

ICI REPOSE VINCENT VAN GOGH
1853—1890

I

Gare du Nord, 9.56 AUVERS DIRECT:
Having the get-up-and-go to make the journey is
    what matters –
Copping on that it is a *day-trip*
As well as a *pèlerinage*
To the grave of a hero who took his own life
But who did not commit suicide;
The accidental company of two young women
In the same train carriage
Holding hands, kissing, gossiping
Ten to the dozen, ten to the dozen
The way young lovers do;
"Lesbians in their loveliness";
The automobile mechanic, six feet six of him,
With his tin box of watercolour paints, his sketch
    pads,
His fold-up stool, his rucksack of litres of water –
All day he'll sit at the grave impervious
To the bad manners of some, the courtesy of others;
The seventy-year-old Irishman in a green baseball
    cap,
A shamrock on its crest above its visor,
Around his neck
A Nikon camera weighing half a kilo;
Discreet but decisive in his picture-making.

On a scorching hot day of thirty degrees
Up on the plateau of golden wheat fields
Under the whirling, swooping crows
Where there is no shelter from the sun
A cry of a man rang out and a shot was heard:
I see in my members another law
At war with the law of my mind.

II

Back at the Gare du Nord on the 18.18 AUVERS
   DIRECT
The day trippers – even the young lovers –
Are too fatigued to speak – too fatigued almost to
   crawl
The tunnels of the metro, splitting up
To seek out the different lines with different termini,
Place d'Italie, Porte d'Orléans, Porte de Clignancourt.

In the Place de l'Estrapade in the 5th *arrondissement*
By a small, three-tiered, wrought-iron, green-painted
   fountain
With six spouts and a circular granite rim
In the shade of twelve paulownia trees,
Large, widespread, translucent emerald leaves,
Incarnations of their blue flowers over,
Long-legged trunks so lean, so spare,
Oriental trees,
Two day trippers to the ivy-duvet'd grave in Auvers-
   sur-Oise,
Where two brothers sleep back to back,

Their feet facing south,
Crouch on a wrought-iron, green-timbered bench in
    silence,
Watching children tightrope-walking on the rim
Of the fountain, two other vagrants with bottles of
    red wine
Having a quiet, tranquil, calm, intense dialogue,
Two Arab women in veils, mother and daughter
With seven-year-old son.
I close my eyes and listen to the fountain –
To those other voices Arab women know
And that light-starved man from the black north:
I see in my members another law
At war with the law of my mind.

The Birth of Arthur Lev Drummond, 25 May 2008

I

God strikes a match and lights
   The candle of your soul
And in the sanctuary of your home
   Deep in the trees
On the shores of the Tang river
   In the navel of Ireland
Plants you in a rack of the chapel
   Of time and eternity.

II

Up the lane the postwoman came
In the bliss-inducing rain,
Pushing her bicycle to deliver you
In your sealed envelope –
Special delivery from outer space.

What news do you bring? – *we* cry.
I am the news – *you* cry.
Into her wicker basket a golden Labrador
Flings herself down with dripping sparks.

III

My infant soul is a fountain spilling over,
Splashing, bubbling, gurgling, jetting;
A wrought-iron wildflower;
Nature in the streetscape.

For me the trees have shed their blossom;
Instead they are all pure green leaf alone,
All globe, all heart, all point, all vein,
Sunlight seeping through.

IV

I am a fountain in the rain,
Time nostalgic for eternity.

Now close your eyes and listen to me
As I pour and fly and dive and leap
Like a Russian goalkeeper in his prime,
Like an Irishman in Russia on his horse.

In a heartless world, a newborn heart;
8 lbs, 8ozs at my mother's breast.
Mother of Amiability, pray for him,
Arthur Lev Drummond of Cartron, Ballymahon.

Meeting Kathleen and Philippe Bernard

Lost in the woods of the Bois de Boulogne
I came upon the railway track of "Le Petit Train",
The narrow gauge railway of the children's gardens.
Standing and staring at the narrowness of the railway,
So grassy that I guessed it was probably disused,
Abruptly the train appeared out of the trees,
Out of stands of Scots pines, out of shrines of horse
    chestnuts,
Its engine-driver larger than the engine,
A large swarthy man from Africa
Blowing his horn with testicular authority.
I stopped in my own tracks to watch the train snake
    past,
"Le Petit Train", its open coaches
Dotted with awestruck children,
Until the last coach in whose last seat sat up
A couple in their eighties
Holding hands and smiling and when they spotted
    me,
Calling out my name to me, they waved to me –
Their lost child stranded in the trees –
And we remembered where we had come from,
And who, and where we were now.
FEE–FAW–FUM.
I SMELL THE BLOOD OF AN IRISHMAN.

DR MATTHEW-MIGHTY-GRAIN-OF-SALT-DANTE-
   O'CONNOR.
BOOMLAY, BOOMLAY, BOOMLAY, BOOM.
BEEP-BEEP, BEEP-BEEP.
All my life I have been snaking in and around
Geographies and economies and languages seeking
   you
And now I have traced you!
O my smiling Kathleen! O my smiling Philippe!

14 July 2009

Le Petit Journal Jazz Club, Saint Michel, 10 June 2009

to Michael Coady

Eight o'clock on a mid-June evening raining cats
    and dogs –
Oh let's get in out of this dark day and this rain and
Try this – 53 euro dinner & jazz
In a cellar under the Boulevard Saint Michel.
The guide book – *The Rough Guide to Paris* –
    pronounces:
"These days rather middle-aged and tourist-prone."
How sniffily ageist, covertly racist!
For do not tourists derive from other countries,
    other cultures?
Coady and I are middle-aged and we are tourists
But, as it transpires, we are the only tourists
Of the seventy or so souls there. We are the sole
    tourists
And, of the seventy, a third are in their twenties and
    thirties,
Two thirds like ourselves fifty and over.
Five of the six musicians are mid-middle age,
While the sixth, the trombonist Benny Vaseur,
Must be seventy-five if a day.

Halfway into the dinner and the music
I say to myself: What am I doing here?

What have I done to deserve this?
In the middle of a June evening to be sitting
In the middle of a 99 per cent Parisian audience
Eating good food and listening to six musicians
Making music – impassioned, droll, mournful 1920s
    tunes –
"I Wish I Could Shimmy Like My Sister Kate" –
"Royal Garden Blues" –
"Muskrat Ramble" –
Giving it everything they've got – cases of energy,
    bottles of skill.

For two-and-a-half hours they delight themselves –
    and us –
Making sounds – solo after solo,
Each solo ending with effortless applause:
Little curly-headed Fabrice on clarinet and soprano
    sax;
Old Benny Vaseur, bald, small, dapper
On trombone producing, hat-rabbit-like, a bucket
    mute
To brandish precisely like an old lady cooking;
Tall, slim Eric with the film-star looks
On trumpet, slapping it with a plunger mute;
Sturdy Alain breaking speed records on banjo –
Oh man, but that Alain can sure bang a pluck out of
    his banjo!
Lou Lauprêtre on piano, doing things with his baby
    finger
A pianist wouldn't do in his cockiest dreams;

Michel Marcheteau – a dead ringer for David
    Marcus –
The quiet man with the pencil-line moustache
On tuba – on his tuba solos throwing up quakes
Of closet romanticism and getting always
The longest and loudest and most ebullient applause.
After each solo all six come in together,
Blowing, plucking, strumming,
The whole sound raising the cellar roof-beams,
Infusing the footsteps of the overhead pedestrians
With radioactive A flat, E flat, B flat
And the seven positions of the trombone slide.

And their day jobs? Of the six only old Benny
    Vaseur,
The elder trombonist who plays like a teenager
With a bucket mute weaving the air,
Only Benny lives within the *périphérique*
In a musty, rusty, cosy den in the 5th,
Up seven flights of stairs with no lift:
But his own pad, an inheritance.
The other five all live in the suburbs,
Doing suburban jobs – running a travel agency,
An architectural practice, a panel beaters,
Teaching secondary school, selling insurance –
All dressed differently, casually, shirt and tie.
Sobriety is the name of the game
When the game is wild and the mood is just right.

Petit Déjeuner with Breda

On my last day in Paris
By getting up at the crack
I'd have the canteen to myself;
In my sixty-fourth year I'd be free
To say my private farewells,
My stricken last words
To the city of all our dreams.

About to munch my stale baguette
The swing doors slid open
And there she was
In her slippers and pyjamas,
Her open peignoir,
The pretty Breda from Limerick
Doing a PhD in Business Studies.

Having filled her tray
And without saying a word
She sat down opposite me,
Stoking her silence
Like a veteran fisherman,
Before, without warning,
Giving me a tongue-lashing.

"Do you, as a male, have any idea,
The slightest idea,

What it is like to be a woman?"
She glared at me with the ferocity
Of all of her twenty-three years;
With all of the self-righteousness
Of her murderous innocence.

She seethed and spittle-scoured:
"Every man ought to adore me
But you on your sabbatical in Paris,
Monsieur le Poète,
You failed to adore me,
You failed to give me
The obeisance that is my due.

"So be off with you now to Charles de
     Gaulle,
Go back home to Ireland in the drizzle
To your slummy bachelor pad,
To your pigsty of self-pity.
Be off now with your limp tail
Between your legs,
But remember always my tongue."

Gulping back my vile coffee,
I carried my tray to the trolley
Like an altar boy to the guillotine
And slid it in sideways.
At the door I turned and paused
Hesitantly, very, very hesitantly:
"I will, Breda, I will."

In the Luxembourg Gardens
in the Rain

In the Luxembourg Gardens in the rain
On a Sunday afternoon in midwinter
A monumental figure of despair
Charles Baudelaire stands petrified,
Screaming his screams.

Unexpectedly his screams fade
Until he hears himself eavesdropping
On footfalls of passing joggers:
Their footfalls beaming head-torches
Down deep into his dark belly.

There is something more than consoling –
Something caressing – about the sounds
Perpetrated by feet of streams of joggers:
Their feet slapping the wet mud of pathways,
The incompatible lengths of their strides.

Loping – creeping – racing – shuffling –
Limbering – hopping – crawling – trotting:
If only one female jogger would pause
And wink up at him –
Maybe even twinkle, for five or ten seconds.

But that would be what one should never seek —
The icing on the cake —
And yet one does
If one's name is Charles Baudelaire,
Screaming in the rain.

Car c'est vraiment, Seigneur . . .
That the finest evidence of our innate dignity
As human beings that we can give
Is this scream which we scream from era to era
And which fades away only to the precipitation
   of jogging feet.

Christmas in Paris

That old man in the window of the burger joint – Q –
On the corner of the Boulevard St Michel and the Rue
    Soufflot,
Who is he? With the white hair, the red face?
Night after night between 6 p.m. and 8 p.m.
High in the window?

In his high chair at the counter window of Q
With his "Giant Burger & Frites"
And his big beaker of Sprite with a straw
He has a front row seat
At the Spectacle of Paris.

His days are days of slapstick loneliness
But for these two hours he knows almost bliss:
The thrill of the traffic, the pedestrians;
The streams of headlights of autos;
The feet of thousands of people, the faces.

Except for ocean storms on the west coast of Ireland
He has never seen a spectacle the like of it
At the intersection of Soufflot, Saint-Michel, Gay Lussac,
    Médicis, Monsieur le Prince,
All centred on the roundabout of Place Edmond
    Rostand,
Whose own centre also is a fountain without end.

Such mouths! Such legs! Such spines! Such hips!

The insouciance of the young, the humiliation of the
  aged;

The fashions, the styles, the rags, the riches;

Street lamps, sirens, traffic lights, umbrellas, kiosks;

The ice-cold Sprite stinging his throat after the hot
  burger.

Vive la France! Je me révolte, donc je suis!

The Road to Vétheuil 2009

I walked downhill to the village,
Carefree because I was going to meet her.
Although it was in the dead of winter,
Snow being general all over Normandy.
My road was strewn with gold blossom
And lined with poplars in full flight,
Down ahead of me spires and water.
When I came to her door, I could see her silhouette,
The figure of her, through the misted pane of the door.
As I lifted her knocker, she lifted her latch
And we embraced and we burst out laughing.
I stepped in out of the dark cold of the street
Into the illuminated warmth of her living room.
She stood there, cross-eyed in black
Like a pair of skis thawing out.
I stood there like a snowman in a red scarf
With corks for eyes.
What language do you speak in Lovers Lane?
Who said what, where, when?
What's all this about women's business?
Be careful not to sit on my cosy.
We stood face to face, talking nonsense,
Not having seen one another for six months.
Delighted to be doing that, and that only,
And not being expected to do or say anything else
But simply to be there and nowhere else
Piping absolute, pure, spontaneous song.

Death of a Miniaturist
"He painted small paintings for his friends"

At the crack of dawn one week to the day he died
From a top-storey window of a terraced house
I glimpsed Pat O Faoláin in black Crombie, black fedora
Tiptoeing across black ice on Charleville Mall.
It was as if he had been skating all his life,
A seventeenth-century Dutchman who by one of those
    biblically
Drastic, mundane slashes of fate and circumstance
Found himself having to dwell in Dublin in the late
    twentieth century.
He had his hands deep in his pockets,
A city late edition rolled up under his arm,
By dint of his cello-knees keeping his balance
And his violin-elbows,
His Father Christmas white beard tacking to leeward and
    away.
A gentleman, you would say,
But a player also,
Such casual elegance,
A man of style
From the inside out,
A cove,
A night personage going home at dawn,
Skating black ice under a chalky, pink, amethyst, blue-
    white sky.

Today I Met David Kelly, Actor, in the Street

Today I met David Kelly, actor, in the street
Outside Adam's Fine Art Auctioneers
On Stephen's Green North.
Instantly in the sun we fell to reminiscing
About our dear dead mutual friend Donal McCann,
Who died almost to the day this week ten years ago.
"But Paul, I must tell you about my *father's* funeral.
Well, there he was in his coffin in the hearse, you see,
And, of course, I was in the mourners' car behind.
Now, my *father* was not merely an ordinary man –
He was the most ordinary man in the universe.
He had his name in the newspapers twice –
When he was born and when he died.
But as we drove across the city to Glasnevin
    Cemetery
I noticed passers-by in the streets
Doffing their hats or blessing themselves.
Wasn't that simply absolutely astonishing?
How my father would have been delighted by it!
How he would have deeply appreciated it!
Donal – and I am sure he had a ten-ton hangover –
Came to the removal on the previous night
And – I am sure with an even worse hangover the
    next day –
He came to the funeral and to the cemetery.

I cannot tell you how touched I was by that.
Such immense kindness! Such immense sensitivity!
Oh yes – and you know I was eighty myself last
   Saturday! –
This yoke" – David Kelly, actor, twirls his malacca
   cane
Across his garnet-buttoned, wine-red velvet waistcoat,
Before swaying off into the multitude –
"It used be for style – now it's – it's simply to hold
   me up!"

20 July 2009

June and Ivor

Although he knew his wife was about to die, when she
    died
It was as if he had never expected it, an amputation
Without anaesthetic. That he himself was a physician —
That assuaged by not one catchword of medicine the
    trauma.
Nothing had intimated to him that this was a possibility.
Nothing had so much as prompted that this would be
    the eventuality.
In the week after her death, he could scarcely walk.
He could scarcely stand without seeming to be about
    to topple over.
He could never be certain if he would remain standing.
He could never be certain if when somebody handed
    him something —
A bowl, a book, a bottle of wine — would he hold it or
    drop it?

His stepdaughter lived on an island
In the Indian Ocean, the Republic of Mauritius,
A coral island off the coast of Madagascar.
She encouraged him to fly out and stay with her for a
    month.
Cross-eyed by his own tears, he boarded an aircraft for
    Mauritius.
One day was much the same as the next in Mauritius

In spite of the odd cyclone,
Pleasantly bright, warm, easy-going,
But as before back in Ireland continually he was seeing
    his dead wife
Walking before him or walking behind him.
One day they visited a bird sanctuary, where among the
    birds
A lioness was prowling around and he was invited
To walk alongside the lioness and to stroke her back
And to let her lick his hand
And, odd man out as he always had been, he did as he
    was bid –
This unthinkable deed –
He let the lioness lick his hand.
In that sandpapery, out-of-body moment
He laughed like he had not done since his wife had
    died.
"I can go home now," he laughed to his stepdaughter.

He stepped off the aircraft in Dublin still laughing
And to strangers as well as to friends he would say:
"Did you not know I was a lion? Well, you know it
    now.
My lioness died five months ago, so for me for what
    years are left
There is nothing for it but to love and to work
And to let her lick my hand whenever she wants.
And to let her lick my hand whenever she wants."

The Café Java

Inside the door of the Café Java there is an obelisk
    with an urn
And while she was standing in line for her tall latte
    to take out
She put her arms around the obelisk and laid her
    head on the urn
And smiled – smiled at me sitting in the corner
Peacefully not reading my unopened copy of *The*
    Irish Times,
Instead lapping up the sunlight spilling out all over
    the street outside.
"Do I know you?" I asked her. "No," she replied,
    "you do not know me."

Closing her eyes, she resumed smiling.
Then she straightened up, her curly black hair lying
    down
On each of her broad shoulders.
She put her hands in the pockets of her black velvet
    jacket,
Fondling her euros.
Having collected her tall latte she flew out the door
And I started talking to her ghost ten to the dozen:
"That obelisk, that urn, I know what they mean to
    you
But, look, look at me, old obelisk that I am,

Old urn that I am, brimful of my own ashes,
Next time why not lean on me?
I won't pretend to even notice if you don't want
    me to."

She came flying back into the Café Java
Looking for her M&S bag, which she'd left behind
    her.
As she began to fly back out of the Café Java
She stopped in her tracks and looked me in the
    eyes,
Her broad shoulders, her proud breasts, her
    blooming thighs,
She said: "You look as though you're really enjoying
    the bit of sunshine."
"Yes, yes, yes," I beamed up at her, "how dead right
    you are!"
Adjacent to me three very small, very aged ladies
    were pecking away,
Taking note of every falling crumb.

Charles Brady, Painter

after Veronica Bolay

Man sitting at the bar at noon
Overlooking the sea;
Wearing a tea cosy on his head,
A meat-red tea cosy.

Silence except for him humming
"Cosy!
O my cosy!
How I mind my cosy!

You're not just *looking* at my tea cosy –
You're *staring* at my tea cosy!
You *like* my tea cosy?
Veronica knitted it for me.

They say Veronica does not exist –
That she's apocryphal
But – by the way –
Did I tell you I have cancer?

I do – I have lymphatic cancer.
I can tell you Veronica does exist.
Veronica knitted me the tea cosy
I am wearing on my head.

And now
That's me finished talking for the day.
Time for a taxi, a pot of tea
And work – lovely, lovely work!"

And, with that, he inserted his forefinger
In the loop on top of the tea cosy
And removing the ensemble from his head
Twirled it as he exited the saloon – the
    swing doors swinging to the rhythm of
    his tread.

To Dympna Who Taught Me Online Banking

In the bank on the bridge
She came out from behind her counter
With her hands on her hips
In her pinstripe culottes of red velours
With matching pinstripe jacket of red velours,
Black stockings up to her knees,
And she looked me in the eyes and announced:
"I am going to give you a lesson."

She walked me across to a telephone on a shelf
With a computer terminal beside it and she said:
"Call your Open 24 Hour Number."
I said: "What?"
She sighed: "You mean to say you don't know it?
Look at your Laser card – the number on top."

After I'd made the call and answered to an automated
    voice
She waved her hands over the keyboard
Like a priest over the altar at Mass:
"Now we put up the website and log in,
But to log in you need a Personal Access Number.
Choose any six-digit number.
Secondly, we need your password,
Which must have not more than eight letters –
I suggest an animal."

"Log in," she commanded me, and I log in.
"There you are," she cried merrily, but indignantly
That in the year 2009 a male of the species
Does not know the first thing about online banking.
"Isn't it fun — online banking?" she murmured audibly.

There was a Cross — about eight feet high — timber —
Free-standing beside an ATM —
I have no idea what it could have been doing there.
She snapped: "This wrap keeps getting in the way."
And she tore a mile-long white linen wrap from her bare
    shoulders
And threw it at the Cross, draping it on the crossbar.
"Now, are you satisfied? Have a fun weekend."

Outside on the banks of the Grand Canal
In a May mist, sun seeping through it,
Staring up at the oldest, tallest poplar tree on the canal,
I stroll along the water's edge
Like a Japanese sage on the edge of a waterfall
Making up a scroll:
        TO DYMPNA
                WHO TAUGHT ME
                        ONLINE BANKING

The Lady in Weir's
to Nerys Williams

Dithering outside Weir & Sons on a bright April
   morning,
Grafton Street in spate on high heels and sunglasses,
Pedestrians more inclined to parading than walking,
I was loathe to penetrate the oldest, most upmarket,
   exclusive
Jewellers and silversmiths in Ireland,
Established 1869 by appointment to Queen Victoria.
I slinked in the open door to find myself among
   counters
Of glass cases teeming with sparkling wristwatches
And behind both counters on my left and my right
Throngs of sales assistants and managers.
A small old duchess squeaked, "May I help you?"
It was an enquiry of such brisk, curt texture
I responded despondently, "Yes, my watch strap has
   snapped.
I'm looking for a new watch strap."
She took my watch in her hands like a doctor about
   to take my pulse.
Abruptly her demeanour changed and she cried out,
   "It's a Swatch!
Why didn't you tell me it was a Swatch?
Why of course I have a strap for a Swatch.
I shall be delighted to accommodate you –

To provide you with a strap for your Swatch."
She teetered behind the glass case, fondling my
    Swatch
Like an aged female baboon dandling her duke's
    jewellery.

At first I had thought she was about sixty-nine or
    seventy-one,
But as she ticked with pleasure at the spectacle of
    my Swatch
It dawned on me that she was millions of years old,
That she was Pre-Cambrian, that she was the rock
On which Weir's had been founded (and also,
    perhaps,
The reason that Weir's is not listed in the Yellow
    Pages).
Curtseying to me, she screeched and ran up and
    down
Behind the counter, a brouhaha in the savannah.
Thrusting out before me a tray of straps,
She was displaying to me a litter of exotic fruits.
"Now, which of these straps would you like for your
    Swatch?
There's a red strap, *here's* a yellow strap, *that's* a brown
    strap.
All Swatch straps for Swatch watches.
Ah yes, the black strap, that's a fetching little strap.
It will do very nicely on your Swatch. That
Will be, let me see, yes, if you wouldn't mind, sir,
    please, ah, em, ah 7 euro, sir."

Producing an invoice book, meticulously,
  painstakingly,
She wrote down the details of our transaction:
SWATCH — STRAP — CASH — 7 EURO

Staring me straight in the eyes before shutting her
  own eyes
She stamped the receipt with all the preoccupied
  finesse
Of the leader of the percussion section of the St
  Petersburg Symphony Orchestra:
Weir & Sons with thanks 8 April 2007
"And now, sir, good day. And thank you. Good day."
Not alone did she give me a smile
But she sprinkled me with chortles, revealing to me
  her teeth, all of them,
And permitting me to hear the small, reticent water
  feature of her amusement.
Was it a clockwork waterfall?
Or a source of nature?
Back out on Grafton Street I wanted to enlighten
  everyone.
Everywhere I went and everyone I met
For the rest of that day
I waxed ecstatic about a chink of light in the
  neo-corporate wall of Celtic Tiger Ireland,
About the Pre-Cambrian in Grafton Street in the year
  of 2007 on a bright April morning, the lady in
  Weir's.

The Recession

The bank robbers in the Celtic Tiger era –
I do not mean the gentlemen with the sawn-off
    shotguns –
I mean the double-vent bonus boys –
Brought a reign of terror into the lives
Of the innocent, the elegant, the confused, the
    polite,
Such as the woman passer-by who this morning
    stopped me on Duke Street:
"You wouldn't know me but I knew your father!
I'm eighty-two!
You're so like him! You're just so like him!
Isn't it a simply glorious morning?
And it's not yet even eleven o'clock!
(*Imperious glance at bony wrist*) It's only ten to eleven
On a Saturday morning in the middle of December
And the sun beaming like a toddler on a potty!
The recession! Don't even say the word.
Don't *utter* it.
I lost my pension, the whole jing bang lot
To that gang of tight-bottomed, piotious, creeping
    Jesuses in Allied Irish Banks.
What does it matter?
I am eighty-two and I am as new as a snowdrop.
No, not a snowdrop, a sunflower.

I've just been looking in the window of Cleo's in
    Kildare Street.
Do you know it? She sells Celtic clothes. A gem of
    a shop.
She's got a vase of sunflowers in the middle of the
    window
And, all around it, garments
Of every hue of gold you have ever seen,
Every lunula, every monstrance.
It could be an altar in St Petersburg, Cleo's window,
An iconic boutique, all hand-knitted vestments,
The holiness of the soul's body, no less!
I said to myself: This is ME, this window!
This window is ME!
Cleo's is ME!
And I have four sons who think the world of me,
While over on the north side
Mary Brierly who is only half my age
Is at death's door.
Cancer. Inoperable. Now that's a thing . . .
So nice meeting you, so nice. Bye-ee!"

Morning Ireland, Be Warned!

I was cast as the Angel Gabriel
In the school Christmas play.
Next day when my mother
Asked me to take off my wings
(The Kellehers were coming to lunch –
My wings would only get in the way of things)
I demurred and when she asked me again
I cried out to her, " No, no, Mummy! No, no, no!
I am going to stay being the Angel Gabriel
For all of my life!"
       That was fifty-eight years ago
And this morning as I kneel alone in the chapel
Before the empty cradle in the Christmas crib
I can feel myself again rustling my wings,
Getting ready to announce the news again.
Morning Ireland, be warned!

Mother and Child,
Merrion Square West

That woman squatting on the footpath under the parking
   meter
With her infant son in her lap, who does she think she is?
I suppose she thinks she is the Mother of God!

There should be a law, a bye-law, prohibiting women
From squatting under parking meters in postures
   importuning
Male motorists going about their lawful business.

Is it not bad enough having to fret about clampers
Without having these shawled hags under parking meters,
Having to dodge their blackmailing beggary?

As I dodge away I see a white-haired middle-aged chap
In a blue tweed jacket and mustard corduroy trousers –
One of *them*, you know the sort by the rig-out –

Bending down low over her asking her:
"Where are you from?" When she does not answer him
He asks her again: "Where are you from?"

"Bosnia," she replies, pronouncing it "*Boze-nee-iah*";
She looking sideways at me, her eyes half-closed,
Frightening the daylights out of me like an apparition.

The white-haired chap in blue tweed and mustard cords
Looks round at me and roars at me:
"Why don't you give her something, chump?"

I drop one euro into her beaker,
Afraid that he might thump me in the kisser.
Against my will I drop one euro into her beaker.

Looking away from both of us,
Her eyes almost totally closed, she speaks
As if to a deity in the treetops:

"I am dreaming of my holy child, when he was born
On the roadside and nobody – nobody – noticed
Except, through a railing, a donkey

Whose eyes were so lit up I could see
My child's baby fingers by the light of those eyes,
My child who one day will go to school and college and
    – and – save the world!"

"Did you hear that?" said the other chap.
"Did you hear that?" said the other chap again,
And a third time, roaring it: "Did you hear that?"

I wanted to beg the woman squatting on the footpath
Under the parking meter to beg him to stop it.
Please, Missus, whoever you are, beg him to stop it.

Our Lady of the Parking Meters, have mercy on us!

Forefinger

A man's irresponsible member can also be scary
If not terrifying.
But what is most appalling in a man is his forefinger –
That instrument of admonition, of waging fear,
Of merciless condemnation in the name of making a
    point.

*

One forefinger in particular I recall most of all.
It was on the tarmac of the airport in Managua,
Capital city of Nicaragua, in 1983:
Pope John Paul II, the Polish Pope,
Having descended the steps from his aircraft
And having kissed Nicaraguan soil
He was proceeding down along the line of the
    Nicaraguan government,
The Prime Minister, Daniel Ortega, at his side,
When he halted at the Minister of Education.
A small, frail priest in a black beret
Dropped to his knees to receive the Pope's blessing.

But no blessing was forthcoming from the Polish Pope.
Instead of configuring the sign of love and mercy
In the archetypal style as old as Christ Himself,
The Pope shot out his forefinger like a viper its tongue

And jabbing it, jabbed it again and again
Into the frantic eyes of the small, frail priest
Who was the Minister of Education in the Nicaraguan
  government.
You could see the Pope admonishing the priest
But there was no microphone to relay his words.
Later, it was reported
That he had rebuked the priest for being a government
  minister:
"It is not the business of a priest"
He was reported to have hissed
"To be a government minister!"

For the rest of that day and for the next twenty-two
  years
The Polish Pope's forefinger stalked me night and day,
A long, drawn-out red penis with a manicured violet
  fingernail
Emptying Christianity out of all Church practice.
In those twenty-two years right up to his death
Pope John Paul II's forefinger followed me down
All the back lanes as well as main streets of my life
Until one night I sat up in bed with the sweats
Dye-stamping my pyjamas on my flesh –
There he was leading a baton charge of storm troopers,
His forefinger not only a penis out of control
But a baton being wielded by a berserk commander.
O Karol Wojtyła, may Christ have mercy on you
For I cannot – God forgive me.

Meeting the Poet

On the spur of the moment I pulled into a
　　filling station
For a quick cappuccino to sip at the wheel.
As I hastened back out of the shop towards my
　　car
The poet drove up and rolled down his window.
I stopped; he smiled; there was a silence
Before he took my free hand in his two hands
And kissed it. He did not speak.
I bent down low and kissing the back of his
　　hand
I stepped back. I did not speak.
Shaking his head, he drove slowly away.
Gaping at the froth of my cappuccino
I emptied it down a drain, tossing my beaker
　　into a bin.
Whatever it is that is the extinction of sin.

Kate La Touche

William Orpen wrote: *French Women are Tough* –
A caption to his drawing of a naked Yvonne
    cuffing a naked William.
But the gentlest woman I have ever known
As well as being tough
Was a La Touche,
An Irish French Woman,
A descendant of the non-conformist Huguenots
Interred in the pocket graveyard in Merrion
    Row, Dublin,
Between the high gable walls
Of the Department of Finance and the
    McDonnell & Dixon office block.
She embodies gentleness, Kate La Touche,
Frankness
As well as beauty and truth,
The bit between her teeth,
All gaiety, all gravitas, all blue, all grey.
This April morning the pocket graveyard has
    stepped out
As if amiably for her:
Bluebells, hostas, box, gravel;
A few limestone headstones.
O where are you today, Kate La Touche?
In and out of history
Fully clothed

Or not fully clothed
Cuffing
A naked William,
Sweet non-conformist
Toughing it out
Like cherry blossom!

A Man Besotted by his Batch

In the Spar supermarket on Merrion Row,
Opposite O'Donoghue's public house,
When I presented my basket at the checkout
To my dismay it was taken
Not by one of the many Polish girls manning
    the checkouts
But by a short, stocky, curly, red-headed male
    Dubliner
Screeching to himself "The Auld Triangle"
By Brendan Behan:
And the auld triangle
Goes jingle jangle
All along the banks
Of the Royal Canal.
He was all bonhomie but not excessively.
He commented on my every item,
But when I handed him
My batch loaf of bread
He seized-up, swooned, swayed, roared:
"Jasus!" he exploded. "A batch!"
He continued as if performing an aria in the
    Messiah
"When I was in Australia – and don't get me
    wrong –
I loved it in Australia – every Dublin man
Should spend time in Australia –

But the one thing I missed was my batch.
After seven years in Perth – Jasus!
You should see the women in Perth! –
When I came home to Dublin
The first thing I did was to go out
And buy myself a batch
And I came back with my batch
And I smeared two slices with dollops of
    butter
And I made one gorgeous ham sandwich.
The women of Perth, O Jasus, forgive me,
But there's nothing – not even a Perth
    woman –
To beat a batch. Thank you, sir. Have a
    good day."

Michael Longley's Last Poetry Reading

On the occasion of his last poetry reading
As Ireland Professor of Poetry
In Trinity College Dublin,
While in the tiered lecture theatre
The expectant audience perched
Chattering on its boughs,
Michael Longley sent word
That he himself could not attend
On account of being detained
By two Vermeer women
In a nearby restaurant
Called The Pig's Ear,
But that in his place
A pair of red braces
Would give the reading.

And so it was
For almost one hour
On an empty stage
A pair of red braces
With a white beard
Gave the most memorable
Reading ever given in Trinity College –
A red robin on a telegraph wire
In a blue sky at dusk

Could not have been
More pitch-perfect, note-acute,
Breast-erect.
Vanished from our cobblestones,
How we shall miss him!

To be Ella or Not to be Ella

The day after they amputated Ella Fitzgerald's legs –
She had diabetes –
One of her admirers exclaimed to her: "I'm so sorry!"
Ella cried: "I don't sing with my legs, I sing with my
  voice!"

A Cast-Iron Excuse

Sorry I cannot come to your reading tonight.
I have to go to the South Pole.

Sandymount Green

Driving past Sandymount Green at 6 a.m. on a
    spring morning
There was a crow on top of the head of Power's
    sculpture of Yeats.
It took my eye, that and the over-powering
    topographical feature
That the Green is heart-shaped with black palings
    under chestnuts
And at the heart of the heart of it
Lying together in the grass in the middle of the
    Green
The two down-and-outs of the night before,
With their carrier bags of bottles and socks,
In one another's arms
As if they had fallen out of the solitary palm tree
Into the middle of their own dream,
Cheek to cheek in the sunlight,
The rising sun lighting up their sleeping faces,
Their anoraks, their tracksuits, their trainers.
And you – you tell me that they have a drink
    problem.
Well, they have one another while you, you have
    no one.

Achill Island Postman

Driving up the rocky track to the six-barred gate
Of the cottage on the mountain on the western sea
I look to see if atop the locked black mailbox
Is there a nugget of white quartz?

The sort of man the postman is, Tony Grealis:
If he has been here and dropped mail in my box
He picks up a nugget of white quartz
From the churned-up, washed-out earth,

Placing it on top of the locked black mailbox.
Every day five days a week in snowstorms or anticyclones
He zips up and down the mountains and the valleys,
The boreens, the braes, the right of ways

In a dinky green van delivering the mail –
He who lives for his family, his wife and his children
And following Premier League soccer on Sky TV.
Quartz – the only metamorphic icon we have for the soul

And the life of the soul. Ireland
Is chock-a-block with greedy, sneaky, cut-throat,
    vainglorious men
But the postman is somebody else – a one-man rescue
    service,
His throwaway laughter glittering on the black horizon.

1950s Boat
after John McHugh

Prowling through the halls of the annual RHA Exhibition
In the heart of Dublin at the seat of power,
At the top of the staircase I got a fright
For there stood a tall, half-naked woman balancing on one
  leg,
Holding in her arms as if she possessed it
A most delicate, anger-sharp sculpture,
A photographer on his knees on the floor under her,
Arching her breasts for him as if she, too, had been
  sculpted,
Sculpted by Rodin in the death throes of his romance
  with sculpture.

What she was holding in her arms – no, not holding
But embracing – was a piece of the wreckage
Of a 1950s boat washed up on a western shore
In the cove of Dooagh, a Zorba the Greek cove
As much out of the Greek islands
As out of the west of Ireland,
A piece of a boat's soul, a slice of its hull,
The plumage of five spars nailed together,
Black tarred feathers glistening wet after all these decades.

Yet in spite of the tragedy of her womanhood,
All her vulnerable pride,

95

The shock of her adrenalin,
The euphoria of her grief,
She was keeping her balance on that one terracotta leg
Sheer as bog deal from prehistoric forests
In her one rust-brown *à la mode* high-heel shoe –
O where was its pair?
Her petrol-pump platforms from New York City.

She who once fished off the coasts of Newfoundland
Now so high she is banking over Labrador.
Not since the Bantry Boat was carved
On the Kilnaruane Pillar Stone in the ninth century
Has such sculpture sung in the halls of power;
She cannot help but point the finger at the Bank of
    Ireland:
YOU DID THIS TO ME
I AM NOT A MODEL
LOOK AT ME

Woman in flight at an angle to the universe,
1950s boat person, emigrant, refugee,
Somersaulting, diving, soaring to her fate!
And, as if I, her weeper, was a bundle of her
    Grandmother's knitting
Laid aside in an ebb tide of daydreaming
On her green work table, she whispers to me:
 "I was the First Woman on the Moon;
I was the First Woman on Achill Island."

18 July 2009

At the Grave of Michael Carr

Asleep face upwards beside his wife,
Feet facing west,
Michael Carr at last has found his rest:

Facing the setting sun in Hy-Brasil,
The mountains, the sea, the same panorama
As from their own home in Dookinella.

After all the anxiety of sickness,
All its humiliation, all its fear,
His hands have found their place

One over the other, beside
His wife Kattie whose hands like his
Were courageous hands

Broad and keen for work;
That could lift sacks
Or sow the most reticent seed.

On a soft afternoon in late May
In Slievemore Cemetery
Next to the Deserted Village

The quartz boulder known as "the Star"
High up on the mountain
Is doused in mist.

Two weeks and two days ago
At 2.40 a.m. in the morning
He drew his last breath.

His daughter described that last breath
As containing all of his seventy-nine years,
All of his labours, all of his journeys.

In rhododendron-time, bog-cotton time,
    yellow iris-time, wild rhubarb-time,
Gorse-time, arum lily-time, hawthorn-time,
    lamb-time,
Michael Carr died in his own bed

With his family all around him,
His son, his two daughters, their spouses,
Midwives birthing their father into death.

In the throes of sickness in hospital
I said to Michael Carr:
"Your children are wonderful people."

Stricken, he raised up his head:
"They're powerful, Paul, powerful.
They never close their eyes."

The rain is easing and the sun
Across Keel Lough is lighting up
Michael Carr's cottage in Dookinella;

Amidst the black and the grey clouds,
The breeze fresh like himself,
Up in the sky bits of jigsaw blue.

Look – a brightening in the south-west!
That surely is who and what he was –
A brightening in the skies on days of blackest
    rain and coldest shores.

He and his wife sea-deep in their silence –
Peace of silence, peace
Of selflessness, gentleness, patience.

The banging of a car door –
Distant voices –
Visitors to the Deserted Village.

I, a pilgrim to his newly dug grave
Who had the good fortune over the years
To sit on his sofa and roll about in his mirth:

To watch him sitting in his armchair
In plaid shirt, woolly hat, looking out
At the Great Performance of the Ocean and
    the Strand;

To have tea and biscuits in his living room;
To talk with him of chiropodists, Germans
   and how to cook steak;
To loiter at his gate with him

Overlooking the small lake of reeds
With the same two swans on it, year in, year
   out,
Generations of cygnets come and gone;

As a last farewell talking weather with him,
Isobar-aficionado, cold-front expert,
   new-moon man,
Anti-cyclone prophet, diviner of winds.

As I sit here at his grave it wouldn't surprise
   me
To glimpse him kneeling at someone else's
   grave
With a bucket and spade – doing a neighbour
   a favour.

He was a great man for knocking about
Around corners of gables and sheds
Doing odd jobs for neighbours and family

When he wasn't high up in his own
   mountain
In the depths of the bog,
Digging turf, footing it, clamping it, saving it.

Child of hard times at the sea's edge,
Forever playful, forever working hard;
Child who did not disown his own
    innocence.

"Peace go with you, Paul" I hear his
Staked-with-silences sean-nós voice
Call after me as I clang shut the Eternity gate.

Michael Carr has gone home to God.

22 May 2009

Slievemore Cemetery Headstones

I

KATTIE CARR 1929–1995

She is my song, my turf-stack, my whitewashed wall.
She is my house in the hill up above me.
She is my young woman facing west.
She is my seashell I place to my ear.
She is my ocean I go to sleep and wake up to.

II

MICHAEL CARR 1929–2009

He is my man across the Irish Sea,
My hero of fidelity, who every Friday
Sends me home his wages to rear our family.
Stepping off the bus at the crossroads with his suitcase,
His cardboard boxes of dolls, a sailboat, a tricycle.
He is home now for good, beside me forever.

Caught Out

Face to face with a lamb
On a spring evening at twilight
I have nowhere to hide

Black legs, black ears,
White Babygro,
Two black eyes peer up at me

I feel as guilty
As if caught out by my granddaughter
Telling her a lie.

The Children of the Land of Dreams

In the fourteenth century that alpha Englishman
John Wycliffe, translator, reformer,
Pointing west to Ireland, admonished:
"Go you there, go you to its western sea,
Stand you on the cliff of the cosmos,
The black, black cliff of the cosmos
Over which, if you fall,
You will fall into bottomless blackness."

For ten thousand years the rain
Has been making us what we are
On the west coast of Ireland
In the County of Mayo,
Rain black as bottomlessness
Up-spouting from the western sea,
The rain, or the overcast skies
That bundle up the rain in their black shawls,
So that today, tonight,
All that you can see of us
Is a black mass of faces
Without eyes, without mouths,
Silent, monosyllabic
Pews of pessimism,
Generations of potato drills
That have failed us.
That is why, therefore,

It takes but a fingernail of sunlight
To rip open our bodies and souls,
Such affection, such laughter,
Such exuberance, such delight,
Such bubbly drollery,
Such pent-up courtesy,
Such giddy gossip,
Such pathetic palaver,
Such respect, such tenderness,
Such patience, such gentleness,
Such good-natured hysteria,
Such stuttering charity
That we are known the world over
As the children of the land of dreams.

Your father was exceedingly sad
But he was not all bad.

Oaxaca

I

It would not be right to say I was homeless for most of my life, but one way or another I never had a home of my own until when I was sixty-two I built a small single-storey dwelling at the foot of a mountain on the furthermost western coast of Ireland on the furthermost western coast of Europe. I had been sleeping alone in it for three weeks when, on a showery Saturday June afternoon, a man in a 1994 beat-up Mercedes-Benz drove up the sheep track with the driver's window rolled down and a smile in his eyes. He swung the car round, switched off the ignition and got out. He held a bundle of cloth under his arm, which he took in his two hands and threw at me. I caught it. It was a Mexican wrap the size of a king-size bedspread. I recognised it immediately as being the cover of the large sofa in his own home in the south-east, and I remembered him telling me years ago how he had bought it in Oaxaca when he had travelled to Oaxaca to his friend Francisco's wedding. "But," I remonstrated, "you can't . . ." He stopped me: "A gift from my home to your home." He lay down to rest for an hour after his six-hour car journey and I spread the Oaxaca wrap over the armchair the far side of the fireplace and tucked it in at the sides and spread it so that it hung evenly at each side, at the back and at the front so that its golden tassels hung in a straight line a centimetre above the floor-line. I sat down opposite it and stared at its earth colours; at its wide, beaded stripes of earth colours; red, orange, green, yellow, blue, all culminating in those golden tassels grazing the newly laid, satin-varnished, semi-oak floor. I stared in amazement at it.

II

Is not that the chair you sit in?
No, that is the chair I look at.

Anxiouser and anxiouser I get
As the years chop past;
Nothing brings peace,
Nothing contentment
Except the spectacle of that chair
The far side of the fireplace
Empty, imperviously empty.

Is not that the chair you sit in?
No, that is the chair I look at.

Chair flowering with emptiness,
Chair brimful of magnanimity,
Its multicoloured selflessness
Hanging loose with threads
Of affection, loyalty, generosity
Than which there is no more remedial force
In the face of ignorance and spite.

Is not that the chair you sit in?
No, that is the chair I look at.

When we go, our descendants strip
Our chairs of their covers,
Oblivious of their origins,
Forgetful of their colours.
My Oaxaca wrap will be
Wrapped round me in the ground,
Nobody knowing a thing about me.

Is not that the chair you sit in?
No, that is the chair I look at.

At the True Romance Cinema

after Oliver Comerford

A filling station with pumps and lights.
A plantation of fir trees.
A T-junction with a STOP sign.
An after-rain highway with not an automobile
    to be seen.
Where are we?
We're at the True Romance Cinema.
Home at last.

Life Guard

I was driving along the deserted roads of the north island when I turned a bend to see down below me on the edge of a black, choppy ocean, a golden strand which also was deserted except that on a sandhill at one end a young woman in red shorts and red zip-top was standing on tiptoes at a high, steel flagpole, close up to it, hauling on a chain. She was raising a flag – the red-and-yellow flag that signals it is safe to swim in these parts in spite of the ocean being black and choppy. I looked at my watch. It was twelve noon exactly. Her job for the next six-and-a-half hours would be to stand guard over anyone who might come to this deserted golden strand to swim in these black, choppy waters.

I thought of my togs and towel in the car boot. I thought better of it.

She was concentrating wholly on the task in hand, the sleeves of her red zip-top rolled up, her long, fair hair blowing in the gale, hauling hard on the chain, dragging up the flapping cotton of the flag. She could have been in the act of hanging a man and I was so out of my skin that I wished it was the case that actually she was stringing up a man and that that man was me. It might have brought a bit of intimacy back into my life.

The Clothes Line

I'm sixty-four and do you know why it is
When there's a bit of sun I sit out
On a kitchen chair in the yard beside the clothes line?
The clothes on the clothes line
Keep me company:
A pair of white chinos leaping up and down
In a whirling breeze;
A blue bath towel wrapping itself around itself;
Two black T-shirts bragging their bare black chests;
Two pairs of black boxer shorts
Crinkling slightly, their careers almost over;
A red jumper hanging dead, as if playing dead;
Two pairs of black socks open-mouthed like four drunk
    bores;
Striped pyjama bottoms giving me the two fingers,
Their top facing down the black TV dish over my head,
Yet seeming to trumpet at me through each trunk-like
    arm: WATCH IT!

After sixty-four years of companionship and conviviality,
On a summer's day
These are my friends – the friends I have left –
My clothes on the clothes line –
And even if they are – so to speak – silent friends –
Their arms, their legs, their torsos
Keep me company for an hour or two
And they are charitable enough to overlook my mortality.

Achill Island Tourist Spots No. 6

A man stopped me on the rocks and pointed:
"Do you see that house up there?
The one with the broken windows and the water
     tank,
The old house behind the new house,
That's the house where Graham Greene –
The lad that wrote all the books –
That's the house where he used play hokey-pokey,
Screaming at the top of his voice, mad for it,
'I want to be always filling up your turf bucket!'"
"Is that so?" I replied. "Is that so?
I didn't know Graham Greene played hokey-
     pokey."
"Well he did and what is more
It was my grandmother that rented out
The house to him and every year
He used come all the way over from England
Or France or one of them places
To play hokey-pokey in my grandmother's house
And he'd play hokey-pokey in it all the day long
Until the geese crossed back over the road
And, after a few scoops in the pub,
All the night long into the next day and the next.
He did nothing else in that house
Except play hokey-pokey
And stare out the window at Slievemore
     Mountain.

They used say he was a fierce man for the hokey-
pokey
And for staring out the window at Slievemore
Mountain.
Of course the lady that was in it –
And I suppose there would have to have been a
lady in it –
Sure nobody remembers *her* name at all,
Nobody gives a thrawneen about her and why
would they?
Wasn't it him that wrote all the books?
The hokey-pokey lad that my grandmother
Used rent out the house to every year
And you can bet she got a few quid from him,
too, for it."

Flotsam

after Margaret Morrisson

In the laboratory of the space station
At the head pathologist's microscope
Awed by the texture of a tumour,
I in my not–guilty hooves, my not-guilty neck,
To the strains
Of Beethoven's "Ode to Joy",
I am going,
A lamb to the slaughter.

Michael Dan Gallagher Down
at the Sound, 10.30 a.m.

"You're looking great – are you going to a wedding?"
"O God no – I'm coming back from a wake."

Passing Through
after Veronica Bolay

There was a girl and she was twelve years old
On tiptoes on the north shore at the tide-line;
Her hands on her hips, her long brown hair
Streaming down the back of her white frock.

Not a single other creature on the shore,
Not a single vessel on the ocean,
She was jutting out there as if for ever
Facing out to sea, all her life ahead of her –

Out there, up there, in here,
The Heligoland Bight, the North Frisian Islands;
Erosion, shallows, pasture, cattle;
Dreams that were all memories of dreams.

Around her all of her twelve years,
All those twelve years of hers passing through,
All those lionesses of her twelve years,
All those meditations of twelve years being a girl.

Twelve thousand feet above her floated a cloud in blue
Inside which lay sleeping a twelve-year-old girl;
Out at sea, 12,000 fathoms deep
She lay floating in all her blood and her bones.

There was a girl and she was twelve years old –
A freckled chameleon:
A girl lion of mood-changing colours:
Last night green-purple, today orange-red.

In houses her favourite rooms were bedrooms
But here was her favourite bedroom of all:
The curved horizon of the ocean.
Behind her an old wickerwork armchair.

She had dragged it down to the shore
Across the sandhills and the dune grass.
Here she would sit for all time.
Who would want her ever to do anything else?

There was a girl and she was twelve years old . . .

Sunny Hill

after Veronica Bolay

Painting quickly at the beginning of the twenty-first
   century
On the north-west coast of Europe,
She gets up with the sun at 4.30 a.m.
Not knowing if anything – anything? – lies ahead.

The sun never rises the same way twice
On the hill in front of her and she knows
That this morning she will have to paint more
   quickly
Than any morning ever before in her life.

How on earth can she do it? Is it possible?
All those zillions of shades of the "high yellow note",
Montbretia-in-the-sky-with-fuchsia!
A symphonic fireworks display of sunniness.

Then she sees the gate at the bottom of the sky
As if for the first time – the same islanded gate in
   the bog
She has been looking at for fifty years –
The gate marooned in spite of its two green roads.

Seeing how she has always failed the gate
She wants to throw herself down in the gateway
And cry out to the gate – "Father! Mother!"
She who is sick unto death of nostalgia.

"O my little grey six-barred gate," she whispers,
Before squeezing tubes of red pigment on to canvas
And painting the grey gate red –
The goldenest red of all black reds.

But all that having been done
Down across the bottom of the canvas,
With what is she to fill up the empty canvas above?
All that sky, all that spilt sunlight?

Not even a pathologist's microscope could depict
Such intricate detail as do her brushes and knives
Of the dawn sky's extra-adrenal paraganglia –
The sky's tumours as a gold mosaic.

Away with her brushes! Away with her knives!
She throws herself face-down on the blue grass.
Facing her own oblivion in the glory of her death
Never has she been so delighted to be who she is.

14 July 2009

Time Stole Away

after Veronica Bolay

I am an aboriginal woman seeking asylum
On the north-west coast of Mayo;
Staying true to my roots
In spite of losing everything.

Listening to nature, watching it
For forty thousand years;
Songlines, women's business,
All around, all about me.

The black, black bogs beyond whom rise
The pink, pink hills;
Sitting out in orange grass when she dies,
Finding her home in nature's wilderness

As if it were paradise – this wilderness
Of moor, bog, mountain. She dies
There right in front of you –
The rust-red chassis of a 1950s tractor

Post-crucifixion in her bones speaking
On her back, knees up, arms crossed:
"I am giving back to you your own wild
    countryside –
The red, red desert of north-west Mayo."

Woman, Outside

after Veronica Bolay

Catching sight of the woman, people cried:
Who does she think she is?
Walking along a country road in June
In a miniskirt in her bare legs.

In a miniskirt, I tell you, in her bare legs!
No stockings, no tights, all airy-fairy!
She — fifty at least, more likely sixty!
Who does she think she is? Herself?

Not merely a mini but a white mini with
     petals.
A violet vest, not a proper top, as if she was a
     young girl
Or a sisterly gazelle in the women's marathon.
She was always a purple woman!

Sauntering along a country road in June.
Not walking — oh no!
Walking would never be pure enough for her.
She was always a saunterer —

Sauntering as if, having spent the modern age
Hanging out the washing on the clothes line
Strung up between two birch trees on the
    mountain
She is free to saunter now and forever more –
    at *her* age!

Who is that outside my window?
Woman, outside.

17 June 2011

Diversity

Hailing from a long line of Protestant tinkers
When I observed a pair of Catholic tinkers
Erect a tiny sky-blue tent on the machair –
The sandy meadow between the beach and the
    road –
Not only did I feel an affinity with them
But I felt ecumenically proud of them.
It was the tiniest, oldest, slimmest
Sky-blue tent you have ever seen,
Nor was it stockaded by camping paraphernalia,
Except for one tiny, ancient, battered, blackened
    old barbecue.
They were a grey-haired, middle-aged couple
A little younger than myself,
With the tanned, creased faces
Of aboriginal people anywhere.
Coming and going in a tiny white van –
How I admired their devotion to tiny things –
They kept to themselves, never
Coming over the marram grass down on to the
    beach.
For six days I walked the beach
And the shallow waters of the tides,
Incoming tides, outgoing tides,
Always passing close to their tiny tent,

Sensuously savouring its primeval, abstemious
    proportions,
The white van almost always absent.
And, then, on the seventh day, the first day of
    continual rain,
They were gone,
Leaving behind them a spectacular mess
Of soggy cardboard packets of barbecue meals,
Milk cartons, used tissues, disposable lighters,
Beer bottles, vodka bottles, plastic cola bottles.
Spectacular?
It was as if they had gathered up all their litter
And in one fling thrown it all up into the sky.
Twenty metres away stood a large, empty litter
    bin.
Gaping around me in infantile rage I cried out:
"Well! That's one way of looking at it!"

Bernie

In memoriam Bernie Bolger (1958–2010)

A blackbird on a wire above the tree-line:
We can see her but we cannot hear her.
What is she doing so far away up there?
All we ask is to hear her song again.

She holds her head high above the tree-line
Over moors of bog cotton and golden furze;
The wind changes, now we can hear her voice;
Her song rising and falling above the tree-line.

"I will never die, come what may:
For in you, my love, I live and in my sons;
Just as you and they were life's gift to me,
You and they now must take me as your gift

That in the niche in the hallway of our home
You will contain in a matryoshka doll
Or in a small round bowl woven of golden straw;
I will never die, come what may."

27 May 2010

Sandymount Strand Keeping Going

to Seamus Heaney on his seventy-second birthday

In the miraculous hour of mid-morning
Walking the promenade of Sandymount Strand,
Gazing out at the sun in splendour on Dublin Bay

After a flock of geese had flown low across the water,
The incoming tide with two hours more to come,
Labradors, collies, spaniels barking in vain,

On the path between the roadway and the bay
Walking from the Esso station at the Martello Tower
South towards the Merrion Gates

Over the tarmacadam where no feet were
Except for the running feet of young middle-aged women
Seeking the fingertip of a newborn king

I met one walking, methodically in measure,
As if on eggshells on electric wires.
He came walking out of the sun high in the sky

So that all I could decipher was a silhouette with hat,
Yet with the unmistakeable posture of his farmer father,
And as I fixed upon the upturned face

That affectionate surprise with which we recognise
The beloved visage of a long-lost friend
I caught the sudden look of the living maestro

Whom I had known some thirty-five years ago
But had never met on these exotic shores.
"Rio!" I exclaimed and with me he joined

In rejoicing in and celebrating Dublin Bay.
We trod the pathway in a springtime patrol.
I said: "Are you facing East?"

He replied: "Yes, I am facing East."
We looked together to our right
Southwards to the sun climbing towards noon.

He said: "To me it is all right of ways,
It is all poems, centuries, meditations
To my spirit appeased but peregrine

Among my granddaughters with my wife,
My daughter, my sons and their wives."
I said: "I am thinking it has been

A strange way to have spent one's life,
Fifty or more years composing poems."
He nodded his head, concelebrated with heart.

He said: "What has it been all about but to . . .
Donner un sens plus pur aux mots de la tribu.
What we must do must be done

On our own. The main thing
Is to write for the joy of it.
The English language belongs to us."

We knew where we had come from, the medieval
    kingdoms
Of the 1940s, the ballrooms where he obeyed his mother's
    pleas
"Be sure and dance with the girls who are not asked."

The sun was at its zenith. In the glittering and sparkling
    bay
He left me with a kind of valediction,
Fading into the whiteout of the angelus bell of the Star of
    the Sea.

My courageous comrade, what good stamina you own!
On what distant shore will you leave your body?
Be it Lake Garda or Erie, it will be close to home.

On Being Collected at the Railway Station in Ennis

Strapping myself into my seat belt, I asked the driver
Who'd been sent by the Committee to collect me at the
    station:
"What line of work are you in, yourself?"
He replied: "Air traffic control."
As he switched on the ignition – O boy but was I pleased!
All my life I've been thinking about air traffic controllers,
How I admire them, these faceless, anonymous people
All over the world who instead of making war
Make it possible for human beings to criss-cross the skies
Of the warring world in peace and extraordinary safety.
At the first roundabout he took his right hand off the
    steering wheel
To invite a circling driver to complete her circle, then
With his left hand he waved to a man on the left
To move out. When we came out of the roundabout
He changed into what I thought was third gear
But in fact was what he called seventh gear and we took
    to the air
Flying low across the new suburban rooftops of Ennis
To regain the road just outside the main gates
Of the Old Ground Hotel in Ennis.
Not only did he drive right up to the door
But he insisted on accompanying me to reception
And checking me in himself on the Committee's behalf.

So quiet, so modest, so unassumingly old-fashioned,
A hidden smile lighting up the features of his face:
The silver moustache, the blue eyes.
Before I had time to thank him, he had disappeared
Off up into the skies of the open, ivy'd doorway.
An official, young, American, fair-haired woman, watching,
  observed to me:
"There are men who make the world go round."

Sick of Acquaintances Who are Know-Alls

Sick of acquaintances who are know-alls
I jump into my car and drive to the sea.
I walk to the cliff, the sea 300 feet below,
The farmer-woman of the ocean
Churning the green and the white,
The tide in and nothing to be seen
Except turbulence and her,
Cosmos empty except for speck
Of container ship on horizon.
How idiotic it would be to jump.
How idiotic it is not to jump.

Staring Out the Window Three Weeks after his Death

On the last day of his life as he lay comatose in the hospital
    bed
I saw that his soul was a hare which was poised
In the long grass of his body, ears pricked.
It sprang toward me and halted and I wondered if it
Could hear me breathing
Or if it could smell my own fear, which was,
Could he but have known it, greater than his
For plainly he was a just and playful man
And just and playful men are as brave as they are rare.
Then his cancer-eroded body appeared to shudder
As if a gust of wind blew through the long grass
And the hare of his soul made a U-turn
And began bounding away from me
Until it disappeared from sight into a dark wood
And I thought – that is the end of that,
I will not be seeing him again.
He died in front of me; no one else was in the room.
My eyes teemed with tears; I could not damp them down.
I stood up to walk around his bed
Only to catch sight again of the hare of his soul
Springing out of the wood into a beachy cove of sunlight
And I thought: Yes, that's how it is going to be from now on.
The hare of his soul always there, when I least expect it;
Popping up out of nowhere, sitting still.

Old Lady in a Wheelbarrow, Haiti, January 2010

after Brenda Fitzsimons, photographer

In the port of Kinsale in the summer of 1948
An old man squeaked along the quays in the sun in
    a wheelbarrow
Wheeled by anyone with a heart to wheel him.
At three years of age to my eyes he was older than
    time,
Unbearably sad, unbearably beautiful,
Unquestionably unconquerable. Although I loved my
    parents
They were puny and petty compared to the old
    man in the wheelbarrow,
Just as yesterday in Port au Prince after the
    earthquake in Haiti
Through the streets of the apocalypse squeaked an
    old lady in a wheelbarrow,
Past a charred skull with its teeth intact smoking a
    cigarette
And a two-storey boutique keeling over, about to
    go down;
An old lady who, although at the end of her tether,
Exuded the same grief, the same dignity, the same
    beauty;
Under her green headscarf her assailed face splashed
    with foliage;

Her right hand held out palm-outward
In supplication but defiance.
Like all the women of Haiti
In defeat she is unconquerable.
Great is her izzat throughout the world.
Being able to see her progress through hell
Under a night sky strewn with petals
I am a child aged three years again –
Teeming with belief in the miracle of life again.
O who when the night of this world is past,
Old Lady of the Wheelbarrow, pray for me.

Wild Life on the Grand Canal

A year and a half ago I bought a minuscule digital camera,
A Lumix, passing through Singapore
On my way home from South Australia to Ireland,
A Panasonic Lumix "MADE IN JAPAN".
But I could never bring myself to use it
Until last Sunday morning, September 20th 2009,
Deserted streets, sunny, mild,
Inexplicably at peace with myself,
Carefree energy in which you feel you can do anything,
I got straight out of bed at 10 a.m.,
Drove straight up from Ringsend to the lock
On the Grand Canal at Baggot Street Bridge,
The Lock of the Three Seats.

I would make a photographic record
Of the Lock of the Three Seats
For my own pleasure,
For no other reason than my own pleasure.
The sort of behaviour you'd expect
From an anal-retentive nutter the like of me –
A female relation's recent assessment of me.

Having photographed the two Patrick Kavanagh seats,
One on either side of the canal,
I turned around to the Percy French seat
Only to find a Japanese lady seated on it,

Reading a book,
A young middle-aged, petite, studious-looking
Japanese lady with short black hair, black spectacles.
I tried to circle around her at a distance
Without her noticing, taking the odd quick snap,
Foolishly thinking that she had not noticed anything
Until she looked up and shone her smile on me,
Showing me a set of perfect white teeth.

Caught in the act, I asked her
If she would mind if I knelt down
At the side-end of her seat in order to photograph
The inscription incised in black in its grey marble.
Again she smiled: "Sir, you must please kneel down."
I knelt down and balancing myself on one knee
Under her face in profile reading her book
I photographed the inscription on the side of the Percy
    French seat:
Remember me is all I ask and yet
If the remembrance prove a task forget.

As I clambered back up to my feet
I caught a glimpse of her book:
The *Selected Poems* of Patrick Kavanagh
In the Penguin Classics paperback edition
Edited and annotated by Antoinette Quinn;
The self-same copy I myself carry
Wherever I am in the world.
In a bedroom in a guest house
In northern Hokkaido in the deep snow,

Placing it on my bedside locker,
Through the night from time to time
I opened it at page 129:
"Lines Written on a Seat on the Grand Canal, Dublin
'Erected to the Memory of Mrs Dermot O'Brien'"
Its opening lines forever on my dying lips:
  O commemorate me where there is water,
  Canal water preferably . . .
When for the third time again she smiled
I wanted to ask her to shoulder me into the canal –
Just a nudge would do the trick –
But once again at the age of sixty-four
My nerve failed me – afraid she might feel
That I was propositioning her,
Which in at least one manner of speaking,
Perhaps two manners of speaking,
I was to all intents and purposes doing.
She said: "Sir, you are brown bear."
I said: "I think, yes, I am brown bear."
She said: "I am Professor of Brown Bear."

I bowed from the elbow to her,
She bowed from the neck,
And I was gone, lost to her
Forever and she to me,
We passers-by forever passing-by.
Wild life.
Brown bear. Brown bear.
Who care! Who care!

Love at Last Sight

We met at Listowel Writers' Week.
Morning, noon and night
She wore pale blue, textures of, bolts of.
Even when she was sporting saffron
Or emerald, her hue was blue.
When it came time
To grimace goodbye, she –
Proffering a mottled hand –
Did complain:
"We will never see each other again."
One of the three most self-contained women
I ever knew. She was eighty-two.

The Old Guy in the Aisle Seat

On the eight hour flight from Dublin to Chicago
I chattered non-stop to the passenger
In the seat inside me. I was on the aisle.

"Am I going mad?" is a question
I have asked myself in the last three years.
More and more I ask myself.

If you were a woman in the inside seat
On an eight-hour flight and the man outside you
In the aisle seat spouted for eight hours

In a monologue as wide as the Mississippi
And as long as the Nile with tributaries
And digressions and flood plains and whatnot

Would you consider him a little – you know?
More than a little?
Maybe even in the process of . . . ?

Of going not stark raving mad but
Of going timidly, fully-clothed to bits?
It was like watching a white-haired waterfall

The key to which has been lost.
It never stops falling but
Goes on and on and on and on and on,

The foam of its toothless grinning
Flecking his jaw,
His eyes hopping up and down in their pigeonholes.

The answer has to be – yes –
I am an old guy going out of my mind
With isolation virginal as an adolescent girl in a
  lobotomy ward on a trolley waiting her slot.

Aristotle with a Bust of Homer

after Rembrandt

Poor Homer!
You poor old boy!
Your exquisite skull!
Your squeaky-new, plasticine frontal lobes!
Your fragile, irreplaceable occipital bone!
Your spotty, slightly sore red nose!
For you I feel the tenderness of the husband
For his bride, all
That spousal grief,
My unworthiness of you –
Of your genius and of your blindness,
Who in your blind state had more vision
Than all the rest of us all together stacked up
Like so many millions of empty plastic chairs.

Outside on Fifth Avenue it was raining cats and
    dogs
And I a beaten man almost too tired to go on.
I did not know it was there – that bust of Homer.
Without thinking and in spite of the adjacent
    gallery attendant
I placed my right hand on the bald nub of his pate
Caressing it with my thumb, anointing it.
Who did I think I was? The Curate
Of Central Park

Laying on hands at baptism or extreme unction?
I think I was looking for support or
For some kind of vindication or consolation
After a lifetime of wandering up and down the
    earth
Constantly making the wrong compromises.

Fingering with my left hand my collar of gold –
A sure sign of my unease, my confusion, my guilt.
In that instant the woman attendant in navy-blue
    trousers
Caught my eye and as quickly looked the other
    way.
She had that resigned look that was sighing:
"I know what you're up to, old man,
But I'll not let on for both of our sakes.
At our age we both need to get all the breaks."
In her face I could see the sparrow of Homer
Flitting about from eye to eye.
I stumbled back out into the rain, tripping over
    myself,
Tottering down six or seven slippery steps of the
    Met,
Having to be helped to my feet by a party of
    Chinese tourists.
How they tittered, Homer, how they tittered!
Where am I to go now in the all-seeing rain?

Valdi

In memory of Valdi MacMahon (1943–2010)

"Valdi, where are you going?"
"I'm going downtown"
She used cry in that high,
   Fragile, wistful,
     Glinting voice of hers.
"Downtown" was Sandymount Village
Across the Green from her home.

Valdi,
No matter what,
Held high her head,
Downtown.

No matter what,
She kept faith
With her lipstick and her rouge,
Downtown.

And if it was not a day for words
She would wink –
A wink of her own devising –
A wink with a sigh in it.

On the darkest, coldest winter days,
On the dullest, greyest, summer days,
She never lost her seaside airs and graces
Downtown
Strolling the shops of her own suburban
    village,
Each step a cosmopolitan toss-up,
Strolling as if always for the first time;
Strolling at a pace all her own
That only her grandchildren
    comprehended;
A pace so wholly out of sympathy with
    her time
That other passers-by would stop to
    behold her,
Lady in a headscarf,
Her stately seaside stroll up and down
The promenade of Sandymount Village,
The pharmacy, the butchers, the
    supermarket,
The hairdressers, the bookshop, the post
    office,
The off-licence, the newsagents, the
    hardware.

Valdi

For whom to be human was the key;
For whom children, family, friends,
    neighbours were all.
Slowly slowly slowly slowly
A meteorite making her way along the
    street:
Valdi –
Downtown Star.

27 November 2011

The Docker at Eighty Walking his Dog in the Snow

Tiptoeing along the river's edge in the snow and the ice
I glimpse him in the trees –
The shrunken, hunched, cloth-capped silhouette
Of the docker at eighty with his red setter Toby.
Not having seen him for a year or more,
I wonder if he has been away.
Hospital? A home?
He lives alone in the cottages.
How hollow-cheeked, gap-toothed he looks in spite of
    that smile.
"You know, I had a wonderful woman for a mother.
During the war, she used talk about Hitler.
Hitler said this, Hitler said that.
Hitler said: 'I'm going to invade Russia.'
Do you know what he says then – says she – he says:
'On the 21st of June I'm going to have my dinner in
    Moscow.'
'Well,' says my mother
'Mr Hitler, you are making a big mistake!'
She loved Russia, my mother. So do I.
I love the Russian music and the Russian books.
The Russian Ballet! Imagine the Russian Ballet!
Of course, we never seen it.
I have the TV but I do not like the TV.
Listen to the wireless. BBC Radio 3.

They do play some wonderful music on it betimes.
I walk everywhere with Toby.
She's a she, but I call her Toby.
I walk out to Booterstown. I like it out there.
Out there you can still feel something British in the air,
Something – something bygone.
I got my very first job out there before I was a docker.
In a garage. The owner was a Mr Hudson.
I was only a chiseller, for God's sake,
But the mechanic who was overseeing me,
Jim Greenan was his name. Jim Greenan!
Do you know something? He was a beautiful man.
Do you know what I mean by beautiful?
He would never do you a bad turn.
He couldn't help it, being kind to a chiseller.
Do you know what I mean? A beautiful human being.
The thing about having a dog –
It's a great way of meeting people,
Especially women. Although Toby's a red setter
She's got golden red hair. An Eyetalian woman
Comes up to me one day and she says:
'What colour do you dye your dog, mister?
I'd like to use the same dye in my hair.'
Wasn't that a compliment!
Even so, Dublin's not the same city she used be.
Not like London – now there's a great city that's still a
    great city
Full of villages, lots of different villages, not like Dublin is
    nowadays –
A fecking great mess all over the place.

Sure in Dublin now you'd have to kick a man to say
  Hello to you!
A long time dead and gone now, Mother Dublin!
All the same the snow and ice do liven up things a bit,
  don't they?
And the bit of brightness is a sweetener. Look after
  yourself.
Take good care of yourself.
I think I'll go on in now and knock back a few pints."
He steps back into the trees, a stick in black, a golden
  redness springing up all about and around him.

Stage Four

in memoriam Helen Barry Moloney

On Ash Wednesday we bade farewell to Helen Barry
   Moloney –
Died aged eighty-five years, stained-glass artist –
In St Mary's Church in Haddington Road,
Across the street and around the corner
From 5 Waterloo Road, where she had lived in her
   top-storey studio flat
For sixty-one years; a four-storey
Georgian terrace house of orange brick facing east,
Its fan-lit door painted blue with brass knocker and brass
   knob.
Her 10 a.m. funeral mass was also the Ash Wednesday
   mass –
Classes of boys and girls from the local schools
Knelt among the mourners, cheeks by jowls.
These were the choirs of angels come
To sing Helen Barry Moloney to her rest.

There was a kind of nobleness about Helen Barry
   Moloney,
Of indomitable gaiety, of gritty integrity,
An uncompromisable spirit, a rebel artist.
As her funeral mass proceeded,
Her early morning 10 a.m. funeral mass,
I saw again the pictures from Sky News

I had been watching at 8 a.m.
Of the blood-ridden, scream-bestrewn warfare in Safiyah,
    Libya –
Young men laying down their lives in front of our eyes
For liberty, just as Helen's own uncle,
Young Kevin Barry, had laid down his life in 1920
That Ireland one day might be free –
Hanged by the British Army on the gallows tree.

As her nephews and grandnephews shouldered her coffin
Down the aisle after mass, tenderly, delicately,
Her pale white coffin tilted on their solicitous shoulders,
A bunch of wild flowers in twine in purple silk,
A bouquet of fresh daffodils golden-yellow,
The young woman solo violinist in the gallery
In triumph like an ancient young sculpture
Played so slowly you could unpick the notes
"It will not be long, love, 'til our wedding day".
Among the wedding guests stood great artists of her era:
Imogen Stuart, Patrick Pye, Michael Kane.
Outside in the dry, bright, sun-blotched, ice-cold day
Fanagan's black hearse was waiting to transport her
To her bridal bed in Glasnevin Cemetery.
The celebrant of her funeral mass was Father Patrick Finn,
    PP.
Out at Glasnevin Cemetery he married her to her spouse,
And as the coffin was lowered the bride entered into
    marriage
Or into what she had always called "Stage Four".
In her last days in her own bed she had told Father Finn

That she was looking forward expectantly to Stage Four.
"All I want," she smiled at him from her own bed in her
　own studio flat
That reminded Father Finn, he told us, of Paris and of
　Paris only,
"All I want is to set foot inside the door of Stage Four.
After that I'd like to help people if they are in need of
　help.
If the Lord Jesus Christ Himself needs help, I will help
　him."

Up the road from the church, crouched on the pavement,
A small, old Bosnian woman shivering, half-weeping,
　half-laughing,
Who, when she looked the other way became a young
　girl,
Young Helen Barry Moloney in Ireland in the 1930s
On the street playing ring-a-ring-a-rosy-O.
"Helen Barry Moloney," Father Finn concluded, "was not
　someone you *met*:
She was someone you *encountered*."

A smile of defiance in adverse weather conditions;
L'audace, encore de l'audace, et toujours de l'audace!
Walking her dog Lara along the Grand Canal;
Negotiating the gangplank of the lock gate;
Pink lipstick, hieratic coiffure, rainbow-knitted gansey;
Sitting under the tallest poplar opposite Patrick
　Kavanagh –
Her brother-in-law –

In bronze on his seat across the water;
A conversation always candid but kindly;
Her short cut home down the old steps of Flemings Place,
A slim canyon of office blocks dwarfed
By a small old woman with her dog going home;
Whose soul was forever young;
In summer sun sitting out on the steps
At the top of her flight of twelve granite steps,
Steep raisers, wide treads,
Fifty-five stairs down from her studio flat,
Delighting in a decent smoke, watching the world go by:
Woodbines, Benson & Hedges, sixty a day;
Opposite the red door of 2 Waterloo Road –
A Georgian mansion of eighteen windows;
She did not care except about what mattered!
She was a bonfire on the shore forever welcoming home
    her hero;
Forever waiting for a baby girl called Helen
To come home in her pram
"Who loved everybody," her mother claimed, "except
That she had a little problem with Hitler."

Our Lady of Stained-Glass Windows;
Our Lady of Rolled-Up Sleeves,
Our Lady of Turned-Up Denim,
Our Lady of Laced-Up Boots,
Our Lady of Cigarettes and Spectacles,
Our Lady of the Tears of Laughter.

9 March 2011

Free Travel Pass

The woman behind the counter hands me my
    Free Travel Pass,
Disgust scrawled all over her face.
I smile at her. I can't help smiling at her.
I say to her: "Thank you, ma'am."
She snaps: "Don't *ma'am* me."
I say: "Oh but I must!
Now I can go anywhere for free
In the Republic of Ireland
And it's all thanks to you!"
She sniffs: "Don't thank *me*."
I cry: "O my good lady, don't say that!"
She crows: "Don't *good lady* me.
If you've no more business here,
The exit door is over there."
I tango out into the street and
Refraining from a hop, skip and jump
I slide into a pharmacy
For a bottle of Night Nurse.
The ambient temperature is minus two degrees.

Having received a lecture on the dangers of
    codeine,
Instead of my credit card
I hand the cocky young female pharmacist
My Free Travel Pass.

She also snaps at me:
"Sir, that's your Free Travel Pass."
"Oh, so it is!" I cry. "Forgive me!
I have only this very morning
Received my Free Travel Pass and
I am so – so hyper – is that the word?
How I'd love to tango with you!"
She glares a very, very PC glare.

I board the Red Line tram to the Point,
Riding the docklands of Dublin like Don
    Quixote
On a camel especially imported from Valladolid.
To any other passenger who will listen
I whisper as surreptitiously as I can,
Seriously surreptitiously:
"You know – I've just been – given – the Free
    Travel Pass!"
Making a slight attempt to brandish it in their
    faces.
I want to share with them my sense of
    Recognition,
Of Affirmation, of Participation –
After sixty-six years of teetering in an island
    called Ireland
On the dark edge of Europe
I am the recipient of a Free Travel Pass!
When, exhausted and furious,
I come to die, if nothing else I can say
"I lived to receive the Free Travel Pass!"

After disembarking at the Point, I trek across the
   East Link Toll Bridge,
Meeting, halfway across, a naked, aged jogger in
   his seventies,
Naked except for a pair of scanty red briefs
In the ambient temperature of minus two degrees.
"By Harry," I cry to him, "but you're a hardy
   man!"
He grins a flamboyantly toothless grin.

I needed badly that lesson in humility.
I needed to be taken down a notch or two.
I walk the rest of the way home along Pigeon
   House Road,
Patting my breast pocket, my Free Travel Pass.
It would be just like you, old boy, to go and
   lose it
On your first day at school.

The Annual January Nervous Breakdown

The annual January nervous breakdown –
Empty streets strewn with bouquets
For suicides wired to railings
And posters of MISSING PERSONS.
Why do Christmas and the Epiphany
Always end in tears – in such bile-black, bilges-beige,
    canary-yellow tears?

Christmas Day this year was such a glorious day
In Dublin city. At noon
On the Samuel Beckett Bridge
Two golden, dark-skinned Tunisians –
A man and a woman – "from Sfax" they told me –
Stopped me and engaged me in conversation
The spontaneity of which was unmarketable,
Their cheerfulness, their delight, their silences,
Their gleaming eyes curious, precious
Like the Eyes in the Stable!
"Is it often like this in Dublin on Christmas Day?"
Each of them asked me
As they gazed up into the blue skies,
As if they had never before in their lives,
Gazing south-east to Libya and Egypt,
Seen up there, high up above themselves, blue skies,

A metallic-silver sun beating down on quaysides of
    piled-up, pearly, sooty ice.
"*Au revoir!*" the woman cried and the man, laughing,
    added:
"Let there be light!"
And I answered them laughing also: "Let there be
    light!"

Between Christmas Day and the Epiphany
There was as much light as there was laughter
And there was as much laughter as there was light.
But when the Three Wise Tramps fell to their knees
They could not get back up onto their feet.
Why could the Three Wise Tramps not get back up
    onto their feet?
O my adored Three Wise Tramps always getting lost,
    always falling down,
Always being late for the birthday of their first
    grandchild!
Is it any real surprise that they wind up outside the
    gates
Of the psychiatric hospital, begging to be admitted?
Over the intercom the Head Psychiatrist deigns to
    communicate:
"Get away out of here, you three anti-social religious
    maniacs!
We will never – do you hear me? – NEVER admit
    you!"